INSIDE

Costa Rica

INSIDE

Costa Rica

Silvia Lara with Tom Barry and Peter Simonson

Resource Center Press
Albuquerque, New Mexico

F ✓
1548.2
.L37
1995

Copyright © Interhemispheric Resource Center, 1995

First Edition, September 1995
ISBN 0-911213-51-1 : $11.95

Production and design by Christopher Givler
Cover design by Carolynne Colby-Schmeltzer / The Resource Center
Cover photo Copyright © Bruno Martina / Impact Visuals

No part of this book may be reproduced, stored in a retrieval system, or transmitted in any form, by any means, including mechanical, electronic, photocopying, recording, or otherwise, without prior written permission of the publisher.

Published by the Interhemispheric Resource Center

Interhemispheric Resource Center
Box 4506 / Albuquerque, New Mexico 87196

Acknowledgements

The economic crisis of the early 1980s produced a number of non-governmental organizations in Costa Rica, many dedicated to social research to benefit less favored groups of the population. The Center of Studies for Social Action (CEPAS) was founded in 1992 with these aims at heart. Although CEPAS closed its doors in September of 1994, its abundant works covering the most important developments in recent Costa Rican history remain. CEPAS' contribution to the understanding of the limits and the possibilities of Costa Rican society will endure not only in libraries and bibliographies, but also in the development of numerous men and women who continue contributing to the social sciences in Costa Rica. This volume is one of the last works accomplished in the framework of this institution.

Inside Costa Rica, like most Resource Center publications, was a collaborative effort that engaged the energies, skills, and creativity of diverse individuals. Chris Givler assumed the task of production and design. Research assistance was provided by Josette Griffiths. Finally, Chuck Hosking lent his eye for detail to the book's final proofing.

Contents

Contents

Figures

Costa Rica

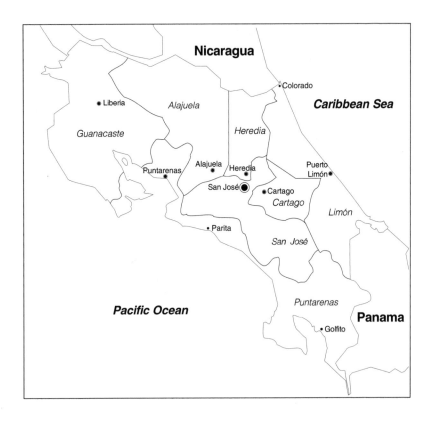

Introduction

Costa Rica is different, and Costa Ricans are proud of it. Statistical indicators of literacy and living conditions explain only part of this difference. It is the other, unquantified qualities that set the *ticos* (common term for Costa Ricans) and their beautiful country apart: taxi cab drivers telling you to fasten your seat belt, warnings about smoking in public places, the diversity of cultural offerings, police stopping to help you change a tire, respect for lines, and a multitude of parks and recreation areas.

Impossible to miss is the extreme pro-U.S. undercurrent in Costa Rican society. Three-time president José "Pepe" Figueres, an avid admirer of the American Way (although also a frequent critic of U.S. foreign policy in Central America), contributed to this fondness for all things "gringo." It also arises from Costa Rica's own feeling of isolation from Latin America.

In many ways, Costa Rica resembles an industrialized nation. Consumerism is a cultural phenomenon. Malls and shopping centers have emerged around the capital city, San José, filling on Sundays with people out for a stroll. Despite the atmosphere of freedom, there is a conformism, passivity, and relative absence of critical thinking that reminds one of the United States. A strong democratic tradition and respect for human rights distinguishes Costa Rica from other countries in its turbulent region, but there is also a marked lack of independent community organization and political participation outside of the electoral process.

The heavy concentration of population in the Central Valley and in particular the greater metropolitan area of San José has resulted in a country of strong contrasts. More than half of the country's population lives in San José, a modern, sprawling city that forms the center of social, cultural, and political activity in Costa Rica. The Costa Ricans who live in the Central Valley are more retiring than *ticos* on the Atlantic and Pacific coasts, where one finds much less introversion and less "proper" language. Throughout the country there exists a degree of order and respect for privacy and law uncommon elsewhere in Central America.

A largely mountainous area, where cross-isthmus travel is difficult except on the few main highways, Costa Rica is a small country (51,000 sq km), not quite as large as West Virginia. It is among the most homogeneous societies in the world. Ninety-seven percent of Costa Ricans are of either European or *mestizo* stock, with little real distinction between the two.

Some 2 percent of Costa Ricans are of African-Caribbean descent. These black residents live mostly on the Atlantic Coast around the port town of Limón. Brought from the West Indies to build railroads and work on the banana plantations of United Fruit, black Costa Ricans were largely confined to the Atlantic coast region until the late 1940s when changes in the country's constitution and travel regulations removed their second-class status. Intermarriage and easier access from San José are among the reasons that the Atlantic coast is gradually losing its Caribbean flavor. The Limón department, although the location of the country's main port, is among the poorest and most neglected in Costa Rica. Costa Rica never had a large native population—one reason why Costa Ricans are generally lighter-skinned than other Central Americans. Today, less than 1 percent of the society is indigenous in origin.

Costa Rica has achieved a 93 percent literacy rate. Higher education is of exceptional quality, but many *ticos* are emigrating because of better-paying opportunities in the United States and other industrialized countries. A country of three million inhabitants, Costa Rica's 2.3 percent annual population growth rate is comparable to other countries of the region.

Costa Ricans are proud of themselves and their nation, and rightly so. Yet this pride is often tinged with racism and an alienating elitism. Despite its many attributes, Costa Rica is not the paradise that government tourist brochures describe. Although the national park system is well advanced, rapid deforestation may mean the country will be importing wood by the end of the century. Hunger and poverty are not the powder kegs of its northern neighbors on the isthmus, but one-tenth of Costa Ricans live in absolute poverty. Malnutrition is increasing, as is obesity. Over one-third of adult women and one-fifth of adult men are dangerously overweight.

Corner bars are almost as common in Costa Rica as the corner *pulpería* (general store). An estimated 17 percent of adult Costa Ricans have drinking problems. Crime is rampant, as the many homes with barred windows and doors (even in the countryside) amply testify. As neoliberal economic principles and neoconservative political thinking have set the tone for political discourse in recent years, so have individualism and a search for easy money come to characterize many social and economic relations.

Costa Rica is a land of legends and myths. It is known as the land of the yeoman farmer, but history only partially affirms this vision of the past. While a historic labor shortage and the territory's distance from the colony's center in Guatemala did give rise to a more democratic division of land and labor, an agroexport oligarchy and merchant elite dominated the country's economy and politics. Thirty-three of the forty-four men who served as president of the country between 1821 and 1970 were descendants of three original colonizers.[1]

Another myth that marks Costa Rica is that it is a land of social peace. Although there is much to support this concept, the commitment to peace oftentimes seems more like public relations than a shared political vision. In the 1980s, the rise of rightwing paramilitary groups that counted on government support, the violent response to popular organizing, the visible rise in militarization, and the country's warm relations with such countries as Taiwan, Israel, El Salvador, and the United States all tarnished the myth of peace that Costa Rica uses to promote foreign tourism and investment.

In Costa Rica, the government has traditionally taken itself seriously as a mediator between classes, and the resulting reforms have created the most egalitarian society in the region. Guarantees of education, pensions, and free health care represent opportunities rare elsewhere in Central America. Yet serious inequities in income and land distribution do exist, and are getting worse. In the mid-1980s the top 10 percent of the society received 37 percent of the wealth while the bottom 10 percent was left with 1.5 percent.[2] The absence of serious land reform has created a large landless peasant population in a countryside with vast tracts of uncultivated land often owned by foreigners or rich city dwellers who like to retire to their ranches for a country weekend.

In 1981 Costa Rica achieved a less enviable distinction among Central Americans. An economic crisis put this touted paradise on the international financial map for being the first underdeveloped country to suspend debt payments. Although the worst of the crisis has passed, its consequences are reshaping the nation. The commitment to broad social welfare within the limits of capitalism that was a national feature since the 1940s began to weaken in the 1980s under international pressure for debt payments and financial restructuring. As a result, large holes began appearing in the safety net carefully woven over three decades of government programs.

From 1982 to 1990 the U.S. Agency for International Development (AID) pumped over $1.3 billion in economic aid into Costa Rica. Supplemented by large loans from the World Bank and the International Monetary Fund (IMF), this injection of foreign capital permitted Costa Rica to survive its economic crisis. The foreign largesse that brought Costa Rica from the brink of collapse to a new period of economic growth had political foundations. The generosity of the United States and the multilateral banks could partly be explained by their interest in maintaining Costa Rica as a showcase of democracy and dependent capitalist development in this region where traditional political structures are crumbling.

But foreign aid and economic recovery came with a price: the imposition of harsh austerity measures, a restructuring of financial priorities, and a revamped development model. The "reforms" imposed in the structural adjustment process run contrary to the economic model of public sector-led modernization that characterized Costa Rica since the early 1940s. A centerpiece of this modernization—the nationalized banking system—is being undermined, and once again the agroexport sector occupies a privileged place in the nation's economic priorities. Also under attack is the country's social service infrastructure, as ministry budgets are being trimmed and many public sector institutions are under foreign and internal pressures to privatize.

The resulting adjustment of the Costa Rican economy has attracted new private investors, primarily foreign, who also insist on certain conditions for their financial commitment. Commenting on this increasing control by international financial institutions and the new wave of control by foreign investors, Costa Rican economist Leonardo Garnier observed, "Without national sovereignty, it makes little sense to talk of democracy."[3]

The country has opened its doors to U.S. investors, land speculators, tourists, and even fugitives from the law. Anything with a U.S. label is valued in Costa Rica. The country has two American Legion posts, and an American Realty Company that specializes in selling Costa Rican real estate to foreigners. There are limits, though. One U.S. citizen, John Hull, was finally indicted in 1989 by a Costa Rican court after the Iran-Contra hearings revealed what many already knew about the rancher's drug-trafficking and arms-running operations with the contras.

The ethos of Costa Rica is eroding and evolving. It is not happening overnight, but Costa Rica is becoming visibly more stratified and divided. Without money available to buy land to appease the landless, the government is responding to rural unrest with repression. Faced with the prospects of unemployment or low-paying jobs, sectors of the urban poor are responding with crime. Where negotiations and concessions once characterized the society, confrontations are becoming endemic.

After two successive administrations by the National Liberation Party (PLN), the 1990s opened to the election of Rafael Calderón Fournier of the Social Christian Unity Party (PUSC). Having seen socioeconomic conditions worsen in the 1980s, Costa Rican voters were ready for a change. But the Calderón administration just gave them more of the same neoliberal economic solutions that stressed the importance of the private sector and downsizing government social services. Despite his populist posturing during the election campaign, President Calderón proved to be deeply committed to a neoliberal philosophy that stressed free trade, export promotion, dominance of the private sector, and a scaled-back public sector.

Under the Calderón government, Costa Rica entered the General Agreement on Tariffs and Trade (GATT) and signed free trade accords with Mexico and the United States. Plans to reduce the government's food allotments to the poor, lay off public employees, and increase utility rates gained the government the good graces of the World Bank, International Monetary Fund, and the U.S. Agency for International Development. Although U.S. economic aid decreased, the government's conservative economic policies opened the doors to increased multilateral funding.

The structural adjustment program that began in the 1980s was even more vigorously pursued by the Calderón government. As a result, the social and economic character of Costa Rica rapidly changed. Instead of promoting local food production and manufacturing for the local or regional market, the government pushed tourism and export-oriented production of vegetables, flowers, and garments. The social contract that once existed between the government and the country's workers and peasants was largely discarded in the interests of cutting the fiscal deficit and tending to the interests of the private sector and international lending agencies.

By the time Calderón vacated the presidency in 1994 it appeared, by some measures at least, that structural adjustment had done the trick. Exports were on the rise and per capita GDP had grown 10 percent since 1990. The trade deficit, however, had seriously widened as the cost and quantity of imports increased and the value of the country's chief exports declined. The more Costa Rica opened up its economy, the more imports flooded in. To finance economic growth the country had raised its external debt by more than 20 percent.

In May 1994 José María Figueres took over the reins of government, restoring the PLN to power. Although he campaigned on promises to resurrect the social democratic platform drafted by his party in the 1950s, the grim specters of rising inflation and burgeoning fiscal deficit immediately appeared to haunt him. International financial organizations hardly gave the new leader a chance to select his cabinet before prodding him to cut the public employment roster and institute a new series of taxes. During his first year in office, Figueres distinguished himself as a leader in regional initiatives for sustainable development and environmental conservation. It seems likely, however, that Figueres, like his predecessor, will see his presidency dragged down by the social and economic consequences of financial structural adjustment, and that Costa Rica will become a more polarized, conflictive nation.

Part 1

Government and Politics

© Steven Rubin/Impact Visuals

Government

Government in Costa Rica is distinguished by its pervasive presence. The degree to which the public sector has assumed responsibility for social welfare (in terms of education, health, and social-assistance programs) is comparable to a similar commitment by many European states. The Costa Rican government is also economically active, having extended public-sector control to such areas as banking, petroleum refining, and utilities. Because of this broad participation in society and the economy, the Costa Rican public sector has been labeled variously as a benefactor state, welfare state, interventionist state, and even as a state capitalist or socialist state.

Since the early 1980s the Costa Rican state has been under attack from within and without. Leading the offensive have been the World Bank, International Monetary Fund (IMF), and the U.S. Agency for International Development (AID)—institutions that have found willing, even enthusiastic allies within the country's business and political community. Excessive public sector spending and state intervention in the economy have been blamed for most of the country's economic ills.

The Reforms and Revolt in the Forties

Big government in Costa Rica began in the 1940s as part of the social reforms initiated by the Social Christian government of Rafael Angel Calderón Guardia. Such reforms as the institution of a labor code, a system of social security, and social assistance programs were an attempt to modernize Costa Rican society. In its attempt to push through these controversial reforms, the Social Christian government counted on the backing of both the Catholic Church under Archbishop Víctor Sanabria and the communist Popular Vanguard Party (PVP).

In 1948 another unlikely coalition overthrew the *calderonistas* after complaints of a fraudulent election in which conservatives were denied the presidency. The conservatives and Social Democrats, led by José Figueres, teamed up to seize state power in what is fondly remembered by some as the "Revolution of 1948." In the 18 months that followed, Figueres put a social democratic imprint on Costa Rican government that has endured for four decades. The social reforms of the *calderonistas* were preserved and extended while new measures, such as the nationalization of banking and the abolition of the army, established the revolutionary thrust of the Figueres leadership. The social democratic character of the new Costa Rican state was further insured by the progressive nature of the Constitution of 1949. As agreed, Figueres ceded power in 1949 to the conservatives, led by candidate Otilio Ulate Blanco. Four years later, Figueres won the presidency as leader of the newly constituted National Liberation Party (PLN).

For three decades, until the late 1970s, government expanded, with public sector investment and spending occupying an ever larger role in the national economy. Within Costa Rica the steady growth of the state met with widespread approval. For the social democrats, it was the necessary result of their development philosophy and anti-oligarchic convictions. For industrialists and the modernizing bourgeoisie, the public sector had been, for the most part, a partner in economic advances in Costa Rica for over 30 years. And for state technocrats, bureaucrats, and the large public sector work force, the benefactor state provided economic security. The state itself set in place an infrastructure of housing, education, and health services that the lower and middle classes came to depend on.

State intervention in the economic sector expanded and evolved in the post-civil war years. The bank nationalization of 1949 established the class character of state interventionism, which succeeded in breaking the traditional economic hold of the agroexport oligarchy while promoting new economic interests, including those of an emerging industrial sector and a rising middle class. Subsidized credit was made available to these dynamic new interests, and the public sector set in place an economic and social infrastructure to accommodate their growth.

In the 1960s government moved (with some ambivalence) to facilitate the national economy's participation in the Central American Common Market by providing industrialists with protective tariffs and by opening up the country to U.S. transnationals. The Costa Rican state became not only a promoter of economic modernization but also a participant. Various corporations were nationalized in the public interest, and in the 1970s government began to promote economic growth by venture capital investment through a new public corporation called the Costa Rica Development Corporation (CODESA).[1]

The other side of state interventionism was the state as a popular benefactor. An expansive bureaucracy was created to meet the education, health, and other basic needs of society. This commitment to the general welfare of the populace stemmed in part from the Social Christian and social democratic ideals held by the country's modernizing ruling class since the 1940s. It was also a reaction to demands by a strong union movement in the 1940s for an increased share of national wealth. In the decades since the 1948 civil war, government social services have been maintained and extended as a conscious attempt to preserve social peace.

The government never encouraged independent organizing by the working class or peasants, and in numerous cases repressed such movements. But rarely has it ignored popular demands. In the interests of pacifying class conflict, the state has often responded with new social programs and new state agencies. In the 1960s its reaction to the problem of increasing landlessness was the creation of the Lands and Colonization Institute. In the 1980s it responded to militant demands for low-income housing with the promise to build 80,000 new homes. In this way, the government has maintained social peace and eased class conflict while reinforcing its own legitimacy. Referring to the capacity of the Costa Rican state to absorb class conflict, Chilean sociologist Diego Palma observed: "The key to Costa Rica is the political ability of its dominant class to impose a system that corresponds to that group's interests, and to have society as a whole accept this system as legitimate." This success is built on the recognition by the political and economic elite that the maintenance of social peace requires some compromise.[2]

For three decades the Costa Rican state developed a certain social contract that, in exchange for social reforms and small favors, guaranteed a relatively passive popular movement. But more than social reforms, the public sector led the way for the transformation and modernization of the productive sector and the modification of the economy's distributive mechanism. Through the intervention of the state, the evolution of Costa Rican society took a direction that was not entirely dictated by market economics. It was the same direction taken by many industrial states, and for many years gave the country an economic and political stability that was the envy of the underdeveloped world. Finally, however, the country's narrow economic base was no longer able to sustain the development model to which it had so long aspired.

The State Under Attack

In the late 1970s the Costa Rican development model began to crack due to widening trade imbalances and budget deficits and deepening balance-of-payments problems. The state was no longer able to pay its bills—opening the way for a conservative free-market or neoliberal attack on the entire social democratic model. The main instruments of this assault on the public sector were the privatization of public sector institutions, an austerity budget that trimmed social services, and the elimination of government subsidies, guarantees, and protections to small farmers.

It is unlikely that neoliberal remedies will ever be fully implemented, given the degree to which such reforms as nationalized banking, social security, public health, and public education have been integrated into Costa Rican society. Nonetheless, a steady but gradual paring away of the reformist state has been underway in Costa Rica.

In his 1989-90 electoral campaign, Rafael Calderón Fournier promised Costa Ricans he would resume the path of social reform initiated by his father Rafael Angel Calderón Guardia in the 1940s. Also seeking to follow in his father's footsteps, José María Figueres (1994-98) campaigned for president on the promise that he would resurrect a development strategy based on social solidarity, equal opportunity, and the concerns of the majority, granting special attention to the renovation of social policy. Once again, these objectives have apparently been postponed—this time in favor of reducing the government's persistent budget deficit. If the paring down of government services and institutions continues, only skin and bones will remain of the benefactor state by the late 1990s.

Structure of Government

National government is divided into three main branches—executive, legislative, and judicial—with the executive branch exercising disproportionate control. Although the Legislative Assembly is well developed and limits presidential power more than in most Latin American nations, there still is a history of excessive rule by executive decree. The Legislative Assembly asserts greater authority, for example, over the approval of foreign aid agreements and loans, out of concern that these package agreements may limit national sovereignty. Although party politics permeates all levels of the state's functioning, the three powers of the republic exercise a considerable degree of independence—a factor that has favored the development of political democracy.

Costa Rica's 1949 Constitution, amended in 1969, limits the president and the deputies of the unicameral Legislative Assembly to four-year terms. Deputies cannot be reelected in consecutive terms, and proposals to allow reelection of the president and to extend the presidential term to five years are regularly introduced to the legislature. The upper ranks of executive government are rounded out by two vice-presidents and a host of ministries and decentralized institutions. The vice-presidents head up two important and recently restored committees, the Economic Council and the Social Council. Since its resurrection, the Social Council has proved to be less active than and largely subordinate to the decisions of its economic counterpart.

Autonomous or decentralized institutions are distinguished on the basis of their business or public service character. Public businesses divide into those that perform financial functions—primarily the state banks—and the non-financial public businesses, including the Costa Rican Petroleum Refinery, the Costa Rican Institute of Electricity, and the Costa Rican Institute of Aqueducts and Sewage. Public service institutions consist of state universities, museums, theaters, and the Costa Rican Social Security Cashier.

The executive ministries coordinate the actions of all those state entities operating within a given policy sector—agriculture, labor, commerce, etc. Some ministries are reorganized whenever a new president takes office, while others, such as health, education, and security, are subject to little change. Recent administrations have taken to creating new ministries to push their particular policy agendas; such was the case with the Ministries of Housing and Settlement, Foreign Commerce, Tourism, and Rural Development. Occasionally agencies are established without formal legislative approval, leaving them to be labeled ministries "without portfolio."

The making of Costa Rican law resides in the hands of the 57-member Legislative Assembly. Deputies also serve on Permanent Commissions (including Treasury, Social, and Judicial Branches, among others) as well as temporary Special Commissions—such as the Commission on Narcotrafficking and the Commission on the Anglo Costarricense Bank—to review bills prior to their arrival in the plenary sessions. In 1993 three "mini-plenary" commissions were created to speed up the approval of bills that do not require a majority vote and that have bogged down in the legislative process.

In 1992 the Legislative Assembly created the office of the People's Defender to collect the complaints of citizens who have been wronged by public officials and to ensure government compliance with the Constitution and other legal agreements endorsed by the state. Elected by the Legislative Assembly to a four-year term, the People's

Defender provides an important resource for Costa Ricans who are protesting instances of police brutality, public utility mismanagement, administrative corruption or any number of random abuses committed by state institutions. Although this Costa Rican-style ombudsman cannot punish offenders, it can advertise to the media occurrences of wrongdoing and advocate for the dismissal of an abusive official. Since its inception the office has vigorously pursued claims against the public sector. Perhaps the most noteworthy case to date was brought against the Ministry of Tourism for failing to abide by environmental protection laws and respect coastal ecological zones in developing the Gulf of Papagayo (on the northern Pacific Coast) for tourism.

The Legislative Assembly also takes responsibility for naming magistrates to the topmost office of the Judicial Branch, the Supreme Court (*Corte Plena*). Justices serve six-year terms but have the possibility of consecutive and unlimited reelection, so they generally occupy their positions for life.

Beyond the Supreme Court, judicial matters are administered by the Chambers of Justice. Chambers One, Two, and Three attend to repeals and revisions in civil, commercial, family, labor, and penal law. A fourth Constitutional Chamber was created in 1989 to ensure the fulfillment of the Public Constitution and to resolve petitions for habeas corpus and amnesty as well as conflicts between government institutions. In carrying out its role, the Constitutional Chamber office has proclaimed the unconstitutionality of numerous laws, codes, and procedures and thus has become the source of much controversy. After the Constitutional Chamber suspended the Transit Law, for example, the Legislative Assembly deliberated for two years before approving a new statute, during which time there was no way to punish infractions or determine legal responsibility in transportation-related disputes.

Judicial bodies hierarchically subordinate to the Chambers of Justice include the tribunals, the courts of justice, and the mayoral districts, whose jurisdictions are defined by territory and constituency. As the primary auxiliary office to the chambers and lower courts, the Office of Judicial Investigation (OIJ) collects legal evidence to back judicial proceedings. In actual practice the department's functions are not as benign as they may seem: the OIJ is better known as a "special police unit" and has been the subject of intense scrutiny since August 1994 when four OIJ officials were accused of assassinating suspected drug-runner Ciro Monge Mena.[3]

Although not technically a power of the republic, the Supreme Tribunal of Elections (TSE) forms a fourth autonomous branch of government, which exercises complete authority over the organization, administration, and vigilance of electoral processes. Created in 1948, two years after the first electoral code was promulgated, the TSE consists of six magistrates who are named by the Supreme Court to six-year terms. They can be reelected in consecutive periods without limit. TSE justices generally are prestigious, respected individuals who enjoy a high degree of credibility among the citizenry. Their power is considerable: in a solemn act held six months before national election day, the president transfers authority over the national security forces to the TSE, preparing the country to elect its leaders. To assist in the processes of suffrage, the Tribunal draws upon its Office of the Civil Register which maintains one of the most complete birth records on file in Latin America.

Regional Politico-administrative Divisions

Descending from the executive branch, government at the regional and local levels in Costa Rica is organized into three distinct tiers: provinces, cantons, and districts. The executive office names governors to each of the country's seven provinces: San José, Alajuela, Cartago, Heredia, Guanacaste, Puntarenas, and Limón. So few are the actual functions fulfilled by governors, however, that most Costa Ricans are unaware of their existence.

Provinces are divided into 81 cantons and each canton into districts. Cantonal government principally consists of a popularly elected Municipal Council whose members, in turn, elect a Municipal Executive. Due to their remoteness, five districts also have created their own governing bodies called District Councils.

In general, the municipalities do not play an active role in national life; since the 1950s, many of their functions have been absorbed by a growing number of state ministries and institutes. They also suffer from a notorious lack of financial and administrative capacity that inhibits their attention to the demands of their constituencies as well as the respect they command from rival government entities. Municipalities are the frequent victims of indiscriminate abuse and authoritarianism on the part of state-level bureaucracy.

The municipalities struggle constantly with the Legislative Assembly to coax a greater piece of the national budgetary pie. Interestingly, popular support for a downward shift of funds and responsibilities is practically nonexistent. It seems that most citizens distrust the ability of municipal government to effectively administer public services and prefer that state ministries oversee such utilities. Due to poor municipal water services, for example, the Costa Rican Institute of Aqueducts and Sewage (A y A) is assuming responsibility for water and sewage facilities in most parts of the country.

Political party maneuvering also has eroded public confidence in the municipalities. Cantonal governments rarely succeed in rallying community organizations and associations to their cause; more likely, they find themselves competing with local groups. Perhaps one exception to this trend involves the cantons located farthest from San José—abandoned by the state's social and infrastructural programs, they have learned to rely upon their own initiative.

Political Parties and Elections

Elections enjoy widespread legitimacy in Costa Rica and are an honored tradition of which citizens are rightly proud. Election politics have found a place in the country's culture, with the whole society joining in the fiesta of flag-waving, car parades, and political debate. The candidates from the country's two leading political parties—the National Liberation Party (PLN) and the Social Christian Unity Party (PUSC)—always stand at center stage during this national celebration and affirmation of Costa Rican democracy. Although 19 percent of voters failed to join in the 1994 elections, voter participation remains one of the highest in Central America.

Modern political history in Costa Rica begins in 1948, the year that José Figueres Ferrer led a "revolution" to contest a fraudulent election and the expanding influence of the communist Popular Vanguard Party (PVP). Contrary to the expectations of the business elite, however, the PLN-led government was not a break with the past but an expansion and deepening of the social reforms initiated by Rafael Angel Calderón Guardia during the 1940s. The PLN promoted an anticommunist populism that, from the beginning, was tempered by anti-oligarchic reforms and social democratic developmentalism. The "statist" and benefactor nature of the 1948 "revolution" truly became apparent when Figueres nationalized the banking system and strengthened social security. Nevertheless, Figueres' coup also brought with it widespread violations of civil liberties of the leftist supporters of Calderón and was regarded by many as a narrowing of the democratic opening.

Since 1953, the year that Figueres was formally elected president as head of the PLN, Costa Rican elections have been characterized by confrontations between the National Liberation Party, known as the *liberacionistas*, and diverse anti-PLN parties and coalitions. In 1983, "opposition" forces coalesced into a single movement, the Social Christian Unity Party (PUSC). From the 1986 elections on, the PLN and

11

PUSC have dominated the electoral stage, inscribing Costa Rican politics with a lasting bipartisanism. The two parties garnered more than 97 percent of the votes in the 1994 electoral contest. The PLN triumphed in seven of the last eleven elections, and governed continually from 1970 to 1978, and from 1982 to 1990.

In 1990, after two successive National Liberation Party (PLN) administrations, the government passed into the hands of the PUSC. Rafael Calderón Fournier succeeded President Oscar Arias after a narrow election victory in which he carried 52 percent of the vote. The elections also gave the PUSC control of the legislature—29 seats for the PUSC against 25 for the outgoing PLN and three for smaller parties. It was the first time since 1953 that the PLN was relegated to minority status in the legislature. (After the 1978 election it was also a minority but joined a majority coalition with other minority members.) Nevertheless the PUSC surrendered power once again in May of 1994 when Rafael Calderón Fournier passed the presidential banner to PLN victor José María Figueres. The moment was packed with symbolism because the adversaries are both direct descendants of the two figures who dominated the events surrounding the 1948 civil conflict.

Although deeply ingrained in Costa Rican culture, political democracy—characterized by regular elections and a tradition of social compromise—bears a superficial quality that threatens to undermine its stability. Many Costa Ricans vote for the *calderonistas* or the *figueristas* not out of any ideological conviction, but simply to uphold family tradition. Once the party flag-waving and actual voting are over, Costa Rican citizens withdraw from the political arena, leaving professional politicians to manage the affairs of the nation.

Democracy and popular participation seem to lose their substance especially during the election campaigns. Sloganeering and personality politics have replaced serious debate. And as if Costa Rican politics were not already enough like national politics in the United States, both parties have taken to hiring top U.S. election consultants to guide their campaigning. Analysts and lay people alike note the rapid deterioration of politics into a contest of television images and popular opinion polls rather than a forum of debate about national priorities.

In recent campaigns, the PUSC and the PLN have devoted special effort to luring voters with the unlikely promise of ending poverty in Costa Rica—what some have dubbed "the political use of poverty." Politicians traditionally ply the electorate with assurances of jobs and land. In the 1994 campaign the major parties also distributed vouchers for public housing, promising to honor the certificates once they won the election.

Hype and hypocrisy contribute to the growing opinion among Costa Ricans that, ideologically speaking, their two major political alternatives are essentially indistinguishable—especially once the campaigning is over and the elected party gets down to governing. Labeling this phenomenon "ideological centrism," Costa Rican sociologist Jorge Rovira Más explains: "Competition between two parties with similar electoral forces intent on making themselves the state power pushes them to the center of the political spectrum, obliging them to reduce their ideological programmatic differences and approximate one another in their campaign offerings. Neither of the two parties can run the risk of alienating the electoral disposition of the voters."[4] To better distinguish the PLN's platform during the 1994 election, party leaders accused PUSC candidates of an extreme "neoliberal" bent. The irony was not lost upon many political analysts who reminded voters that the PLN ushered in the first structural adjustment program that opened up the country to foreign investment.

Costa Ricans are also increasingly critical of an entrenched bipartisan structure that compromises democratic governing in their country. Major systemic biases serve to reinforce the pattern: for example, small political parties are granted limited access to state financing and mass media during election time. Of the 13 million dollars that the government donated to political parties during the 1994 election, nearly 90 percent of it went to the PLN and the PUSC. (By constitutional mandate, the government divvies up the election budget in proportion to the percentage of votes that each party attracts.) Major newspapers and television stations concentrate exclusively on the two dominant parties, rarely inviting smaller parties to participate in debates and interviews.

Ideological centrism and irreversible bipartisanism are clear signs that serious changes are called for if the country is going to sustain its sovereignty and address the needs of its population in the developing global political and economic system. The success of the 1948 "revolution" came from its ability not only to deal with short-term problems but also to create a system of governing and social relations that anticipated future challenges. More than four decades later, financial shortfalls, a rapidly integrating world economy, and the ideological force of neoliberalism are all undermining the traditional structures of the benefactor state and breaking the links between government and society. At risk is the vibrancy of political democracy in Costa Rica and the much vaunted welfare of the Costa Rican people.

National Liberation Party

Until his death in June 1990, José "Don Pepe" Figueres, leader of the 1948 "revolution" against the *calderonistas*, served as the patriarch of the National Liberation Party (PLN). For 34 years, Figueres and the PLN, alternating in power with the opposition party, promoted a modern capitalist democracy with a substantial welfare component. Since 1982, however, the PLN's commitment to social reforms and social services has been counterbalanced by strong neoliberal economic principles.

The party's standard-bearers in recent years, Presidents Luis Alberto Monge and Oscar Arias, ushered in an era of structural adjustment and cutbacks in the public sector. It is difficult, however, to characterize the PLN's politics because of the party's diverse elements, from uncompromising neoliberals like former Central Bank president Eduardo Lizano to more moderate leaders who still adhere to the social vision of Figueres.

Officially, the PLN is a social democratic party and a member of the Socialist International. But its social democratic ideals have been largely shunted aside since 1982 in favor of economic policies advocated by the IMF, World Bank, and AID. Stopping short of complete capitulation to international lenders, the PLN has never entirely embraced or enforced neoliberal solutions, choosing instead a more pragmatic than ideological concept of economic reforms. Nonetheless, the contradictions between the stated social democratic principles of the party and its conservative practices have become increasingly pronounced. Recent PLN-controlled governments have continued touting the merits of the benefactor state, even while instituting structural adjustments.

For a long time, PLN party unity relied on the charismatic leadership of several well-known politicians—but in the 1980s fissures developed. Recriminations and political infighting erupted and reports linking the PLN to drug money began to dismantle its reputation. The party's leadership and direction was vehemently contested by the Liberationist Youth (JL), which advocates a return to the "real social democracy" of the PLN. Now there is also a left-of-center wing of the PLN that strongly opposes further privatization and favors an agricultural policy of food security and assistance to small farmers.

After two terms Costa Rican voters turned the PLN out of office in the 1990 general elections. The PLN's presidential candidate Carlos Manuel Castillo, a respected economist and former government official, had stressed his greater experience and capacity for the presidency while reminding voters that the PLN had led the country out of the economic crisis of the early 1980s. But Castillo was handicapped by deteriorating socioeconomic conditions for the country's poor, a background of party factionalism, public identification of the party with corruption and narcotrafficking, and the lack of a distinct political platform. Many citizens, including some of the party faithful, became increasingly disenchanted with the PLN because it had effectively dropped its long commitment to social democratic developmentalism. As a result, the gap between party leaders and the party's popular base widened ominously during the 1980s. A superior campaign by the PUSC, Castillo's lack of charisma, and voter concern that the PLN was establishing itself as the state party also contributed to Calderón's victory.

The PLN posted five presidential hopefuls in the 1993 party convention: Rolando Araya, nephew of former president Luis Alberto Monge; Margarita Penón, wife of former president Oscar Arias; José María Figueres, son of former president and PLN patriarch José "Don Pepe" Figueres; and José Miguel Corrales and Juan Antillón, both new and unknown voices within the party. Throughout the run-off Figueres was dogged by accusations of ethical misconduct that included his alleged participation in a vigilante death squad during his father's term in office from 1970 to 1974. Reports also surfaced of Figueres' involvement in a fraudulent mining venture and the sale of valueless German bonds to the Costa Rican government.

Despite the host of accusations and doubts swirling about his campaign, Figueres ran away with the PLN presidential nomination. The losing candidates accepted defeat but Penón and Corrales refused to support the victor as the official party candidate. A few days prior to the February 1994 election, former president Oscar Arias gave in to pressures by party leaders and publicly expressed his support for the PLN—but deliberately left Figueres' name unmentioned.

Allegations of corruption also plagued Figueres into the general election in which he faced PUSC candidate Miguel Angel Rodríguez. Campaigning from nearly identical platforms, both candidates resorted to mudslinging the likes of which had rarely been seen in previous presidential elections. As in the PLN primaries, however, Figueres seemed to resist the assaults and rode into the presidency with nearly half of the votes. The PLN won in most of the municipal elections but gained only 28 deputy seats—not enough to ensure control of the legislature (the PUSC won 25 seats in the Legislative Assembly).

Prior to the notoriety that the election gained him, José María Figueres was known primarily for his relation to his father, Don Pepe. For years Figueres dedicated himself entirely to the management of family businesses, never dabbling in politics. Then in 1988 Oscar Arias named him Minister of Agriculture, which was followed not long after by a stint as Foreign Commerce minister. At the conclusion of Arias' term, Figueres left for Harvard University in Boston where he eventually obtained a Master's degree in Public Administration. Figueres burst onto the political scene again following his father's death in 1990 when he announced his plan to run for president.

In his 1993 campaign, Figueres stressed his intent to combat poverty, revive social policy, and protect the natural environment. He promised to oppose the PUSC-initiated structural adjustment programs that had laid off public employees and privatized several state enterprises. Figueres' ability to forge the political consensus that he needs to govern, however, is compromised by a narrow margin of electoral victory and the unstable PLN majority in the Legislative Assembly. More than ever before, a PLN administration confronts a PUSC-led opposition that is organized and openly belligerent to its agenda. Figueres has indicated that he will rely as little as possible on the legislature to push through his reforms, which has engendered further friction between the political factions. Calling for more compromise, former president Luis Alberto Monge warned his colleagues that "in Costa Rica, one can't govern alone."

Despite the haggling among politicians, in the opening months of his presidency, Figueres enjoyed widespread popularity among Costa Ricans. Much of this could be attributed to his iron-hand approach to confronting crime. Soon after taking office Figueres ordered an undercover police unit to patrol the streets of San José and round up the infamous armed youth gangs known as the *chapulines*. Two months later another police operation captured a group of Venezuelan bank robbers who, since the end of 1993, had robbed millions of *colones* from state banks and killed several bank guards. In an unprecedented maneuver, Figueres ordered the criminals deported to their country, superseding judicial authorities and flaunting the established legal norms. Although Figueres was later convicted of violating the constitution, he received unquestioned support from the citizenry, thus appearing democratic in his actions. The incident, however, adds to a developing pattern of unilateral, if not authoritarian, decision-making displayed by Figueres since taking office.

Except for a few aging party stalwarts, Figueres has surrounded himself with a new breed of PLN leaders—friends and followers who are more technocrats than politicians. The younger generation claims to have novel solutions to ancient problems based in the revitalization of social democratic ideals. The displacement of old party faithfuls, however, has created a sense of unease and evoked accusations that Figueres is authoritarian and closed-minded. For example, Figueres' intervention in local deputies' elections—a veritable tradition among Costa Rican presidents—drew intense criticism and was characterized by some as an attempt to undermine democratic procedure within the party.

As PLN aspirants to the presidency gear up for the 1998 election, there are signs that tensions and disputes have not yet dissipated. Less than a year into Figueres' term in office, primary candidate and PLN Secretary General Walter Coto publicly accused the new administration of forsaking its commitment to a social democratic trajectory and succumbing to neoliberal tendencies. The statements sent a wave of protest rumbling through the PLN rank and file until Elías Soley, another presidential hopeful, interceded to mediate between Coto and the president. Criticism has not abated, however, on the part of other presidential contenders. Early polls showed former candidates José Miguel Corrales and Rolando Araya along with Costa Rican Central Bank president Carlos Manuel Castillo in the lead for the presidential primary race.[5]

Social Christian Unity Party

The Social Christian Unity Party (PUSC), led by Rafael Calderón Fournier, represents the bloc of political groups that has alternated power with the PLN during the past forty years. Since 1983 the bloc has functioned as the PUSC, which is a coalition of four parties: the Republican Calderonista Party (PRC), led by Rafael Calderón Fournier; the Democratic Renovation Party (PRD); the Christian Democratic Party (PDC), led by Rafael Grillo Rivera; and the Popular Unity Party (PUP), led by Cristian Tattenbach Iglesias. The coalition backed Rodrigo Carazo in a successful bid for the presidency in 1978 but, as the PUSC, lost two successive election contests in the 1980s. The coalition eventually won the 1990 presidential elections.

Although generally more conservative than the PLN, the PUSC encompasses two distinct political tendencies. The political coalition that the PUSC now represents has historically incorporated the reformist tradition of the 1940s. The ideological right and the private sector elite have also found a home in the PUSC and have come to dominate the party's leadership and policymaking. During the 1980s Calderón and other PUSC leaders were aggressively anti-Sandinista and criticized the PLN's failure to fully implement conservative structural adjustment measures. The PUSC, which represents the more conservative and traditional members of the business elite, calls for complete and rapid restructuring of the reformist state.

The PUSC is a member of the International Democrat Union (IDU), established in 1983 as a global association of conservative political parties, including the Republican Party in the United States. Both the PUSC and the IDU benefited in the 1980s from U.S. government funding channeled through the quasi-private National Endowment for Democracy (NED). In Costa Rica, NED funds went to the Association for the Defense of Freedom and Democracy, a right-wing organization run by PUSC officials.

Ex-President Rafael Calderón Fournier is the son of ex-President Rafael Angel Calderón Guardia (1940-44), who introduced the country's labor code and social security system. But the populist program that won the younger Calderón the election was given short shrift. Once in government, Calderón made his priorities the control of macroeconomic variables and setting public finances in order. Government stability and a profound restructuring of the state were identified as the most important strategies to improve social policy. The most impoverished sector of the population was addressed in concentrated form through programs of social compensation, primarily vouchers for food and housing.

In addition to certain political stability that Calderón achieved during his term in office, the PUSC scored a major accomplishment simply by demonstrating itself as a competent governing force. The Unity coalition that led government between 1978 and 1982 gained the unfortunate reputation as one of the worst administrations in Costa Rica's history. The prevailing opinion during the 1990 elections was that, until then, only the *liberacionistas* had known how to govern, while the PUSC, in its diverse forms, had only known how to play the part of the opposition.

Juan José Trejos Fonseca faced off against Miguel Angel Rodríguez in the 1993 PUSC primary election. Rodríguez—a nationally recognized businessman known for his extensive academic preparation—triumphed over Trejos with nearly 70 percent of the votes, in large part due to the patronage of party leader Rafael Angel Calderón Fournier.

In the 1994 general elections, both the PUSC and the PLN campaigned on promises to address poverty and promote equal opportunity. Miguel Angel Rodríguez proved himself much better prepared, but less charismatic than his PLN opponent José Figueres. Above all, Rodríguez' bourgeois lifestyle provoked skepticism about his supposed commitment to the poor. As a successful businessman, however, he attracted the attention of corporate capitalists hoping to benefit from investment opportunities emerging from structural adjustment.

Drawing upon the legacy of his father and the promise of political change, José María Figueres won the 1994 elections with a margin of only thirty thousand votes (2 percent of the votes). Despite its loss, the PUSC proved itself to be a firmly consolidated political movement. The extent of its electoral base and the firm rooting of party leaders in their communities made the PUSC increasingly similar to the rival PLN—and very different from the coalitions that once characterized the opposition. One remaining difference, however, is that the PUSC has only one lord and master, Rafael Angel Calderón, while leadership in the PLN is more broadly contested.

Suitors to the PUSC's 1998 presidential nomination are already beginning to make their presence known. Although Miguel Angel Rodríguez is likely to figure importantly in the presidential run-offs, history indicates that whomever receives the nod from the party's *cacique*, Calderón, will have the best possibility of filling the post.

Regional Parties, National Minority Parties, and the Left

Since 1931 the Popular Vanguard Party (PVP), the country's communist party, has been in the forefront of the workers' struggles and the leftist movement in Costa Rica. Internal splits, an inability to formulate a popular political agenda, and disastrous labor strikes against the two major U.S. banana companies severely weakened the movement during the 1980s. Fracturing of the PVP resulted in the formation of a new group called the Costa Rican People's Party (PPC).

In the 1986 elections, leftist candidates were divided into two coalitions, People's United and the Popular Alliance, each of which won a deputy seat in the Legislative Assembly. As the 1990 elections approached, the leftist parties attempted to expand their base of support by moving away from strict Marxist-Leninist interpretations and appealing to all popular sectors that were disaffected by the country's conservative direction. But the February run-off dealt the organized left a forceful blow. The PVP and the PPC, presenting a common platform under the banner of People United, was able to gain only a single seat in the Legislative Assembly, from San José. Meanwhile, the two other leftist parties represented in the 1990 election, the Progress Party and the Revolutionary Party of Workers in Struggle, failed to effectively mobilize their few party supporters.

The left has not recovered from its poor performance in 1990. In the 1994 elections, presidential and vice-presidential candidates from the ideological left were nowhere to be seen. The PVP failed to obtain any seats in the legislature (the party received only 1.3 percent of the total votes) and won only 2 out of 545 council seats in the municipalities.

One significant development on the political landscape during the 1993-94 campaign was the emergence of the Democratic Force Party (PFD), a political movement that brought together the Progress

Party, the Patriotic Union Party, the Ecologist Humanist Party and elements of the People's United coalition. Although the party's ideological profile is still unclear, its campaign rhetoric emphasized a commitment to social justice and the intensification of political and economic democracy. The PFD managed to attract votes not simply from the left, but more generally from people discontented with the domination of the majority parties, the PLN and PUSC. Although the PFD received less than 2 percent of the presidential and vice-presidential votes, it captured two chairs in the Legislative Assembly, thus gaining access to state electoral financing and legal permanence as a viable political party.

The number of 1994 votes cast for presidential candidates from parties other than the PLN, the PUSC, and the Democratic Force Party was negligible, less than 1 percent of the total. The provincially oriented Cartaginés Agricultural Union Party (PUAC), founded in 1969, has participated in all seven elections since 1970, gaining single deputy seats in five of them (including that of 1994). The party has proven its commitment to winning through honesty and integrity by making every effort to hold PUAC representatives accountable to the inhabitants of Cartago. The Generaleña Union Party (PUGEN), with its base in the province of Pérez Zeledón in the southern region of the country, gained one deputy in 1990 but failed to obtain any seats in the 1994 elections. The National Agrarian Party (PAN) from the province of Limón was created at the end of the 1980's. In 1990, it won several municipal elections. In 1994 PAN's founder gained a position in the Legislative Assembly, and the party won seven council seats in the Limón province.

The Right

The extreme right wing in Costa Rica is not organized into political parties but instead is represented by various civic and paramilitary groups that are incorporated within the two major political parties, particularly the PUSC. Conservative thought in Costa Rica pervades the mass media and has come to dominate popular political parlance. The extreme right wing considers the PLN to be essentially a socialist party. For the most part, however, ideologically radical positions, whether to the left or the right, have lost their voice in the country in recent years.

Corruption

The integrity of politics and government in Costa Rica has been recently tainted by revelations of high-level corruption, influence-peddling, and association with drug trafficking. The openness of Costa Rican society and the attractiveness of the country itself has long made it a favorite place of exile for international crooks and villains. Their names range from U.S. financier Robert Vesco to Mexican drug figure Caro Quintero and former executioner for the Shah of Iran, Hosjabar Yazdani. The 1989 flight from Costa Rica of rancher and prominent Nicaraguan contra supporter John Hull, who was accused of drug trafficking and gun running, also sullied the reputation of Costa Rica. The international rogues who find a home in Costa Rica often count on favors from members of the political elite. In the late 1980s this high-level corruption came under international scrutiny when high government functionaries and party officials were linked with reputed drug traffickers. A close associate of President Arias was arrested for laundering drug money, and it was revealed in the U.S. Congress that both of the country's leading political parties had accepted large campaign contributions from the Noriega regime of Panama.

In recent years, government financial scandals have done the most to undermine the public's confidence in government officials. The National Emergency Fund, the Appropriations Fund (FODEA), the Agricultural Contingencies Fund (FNCA), and the Certificate of Tributary Credit all have been targets of major embezzling schemes involving government officials. The most noteworthy incident, however, involves the national Anglo Costarricense Bank, which state authorities closed after discovering that bank officials had engaged in speculative investments costing the institution over $100 million in losses. Asked to comment on the Anglo Costarricense Bank corruption, PLN Secretary General Walter Coto observed: "To make yourself a millionaire overnight is a new value that is developing in our society and, for many people, the resources of the state are an opportunity to carry out their dreams of riches."

Since the early 1980s, the dominance of a free-market ideology that favors business, individualism, consumerism, and a "save-your-self-if-you-can" mentality above social welfare has fueled the spread of corruption in government circles. Faced with the prospect of widespread social unrest, the PLN-led government has begun to take a harder line in restoring the ethical behavior of public servants. In September of 1994, a tribunal helped to calm the public's anxiety by jailing and levying millions of *colones* in fines against the Anglo Costarricense Bank directors. The state also vigorously pursued its case against ex-president Luis Alberto Monge (1982-86), who was accused of defrauding the National Emergency Fund of nearly $2 million—funds that he used to furnish his home. Monge was ultimately acquitted (an associate of his was convicted and jailed), but the trial reinforced the message that government corruption would not be tolerated.

Foreign Policy

The foreign policy of Costa Rica has traditionally reflected the Cold War posture of U.S. foreign policy, but the country has occasionally charted a certain degree of independence from Washington. Such was the case during the first three years of the Carazo Odio administration (1978-82). Carazo's support for the Sandinistas, attempts to fortify relations among third world nations, and opposition to IMF structural adjustment created strains between the United States and Costa Rica. The space opened for this independent foreign policy during the Carter administration disappeared with the advent of the Reagan White House.[6]

With Luis Alberto Monge as president, Costa Rica became the pliant ally that the Reagan administration needed for its campaign against Nicaragua. Governmental cooperation was purchased with massive financial assistance from the United States needed to cope with the worst economic crisis since the 1930s. Monge permitted the use of national territory by the Nicaraguan contras, even allowing the collaboration of Costa Rican security forces in the "southern front" mounted by the U.S. to topple the Sandinista government. If important accomplishments can in fact be attributed to the Monge administration, the loss of autonomy and national sovereignty during his government still count against him. By the end of his administration, however, Monge was attempting to stave off U.S. pressure to directly and openly support U.S.-led military aggression against Nicaragua. As a defensive measure, President Monge mobilized popular support for the country's traditional "proclamation of neutrality."

Although President Arias shared Washington's virulent anti-socialist and anti-Sandinista convictions, he saw the futility and counterproductive nature of the contra campaign. Taking advantage of the discredit given to the Reagan administration in the wake of the Iran-Contra affair, Arias took the initiative to push his own peace plan under the motto, "not a second Cuba, nor a second Vietnam." He petitioned Washington to dismantle the contra infrastructure in Costa Rica and began working with congressional Democrats on an alternative foreign policy for the region. Tensions arose between Arias and the White House—with the former advocating a strategy of negotiation and democratization while the latter maintained its allegiance to the contras. U.S. economic aid to Costa Rica was trimmed, and Arias was repeatedly snubbed by Presidents Reagan and Bush. President Arias, for example, was not invited to attend Bush's inauguration. Differences between the Arias and Bush administrations were also evident in the Costa Rican government's failure to applaud the U.S. invasion of Panama.

Beginning in the 1990s with Rafael Calderón Fournier's arrival in office, Costa Rican foreign policy began to change. The electoral defeat of the Sandinistas, the newly-achieved peace accords in El Salvador, and the end of the Cold War all contributed to closing another chapter in the history of regional relations. With discussions (stemming from the Esquipulas accord) of regional disarmament and demilitarization stymied, the Central American presidents refocused their attention on democratization and economic integration as the preconditions for enduring peace and development in Central America. The Calderón administration adopted a more realistic approach towards its influence in the region and ceased to press for the total abolishment of the Central American armies—a task that Arias privately assumed in the form of the Arias Foundation for Human Peace and Progress.

During the Calderón years concerns over foreign trade increasingly prevailed upon foreign policy matters. Although Costa Rica was regularly present at meetings on Central American coordination and integration, it proved to be more interested in bilateral solutions to commerce and debt problems from outside of the region. It was the first country to sign a bilateral free trade agreement with Mexico and to join Washington's Enterprise for the Americas Initiative. Calderón's administration also initiated discussions with Colombia and Venezuela over the possibility of other commercial accords.

By mid-1990 the tensions that occasionally arose between Costa Rica and Washington had diminished as a result of declining U.S. foreign policy interest in the region. The government of Calderón stayed closely aligned with the United States in foreign policy matters. With the Sandinistas voted out of office in neighboring Nicaragua, however, Costa Rica was no longer able to count on generous U.S. economic assistance.[7] Although more successful than other Central American countries, Costa Rica has failed to compensate for diminished U.S. aid with infusions of European assistance.

Perhaps the most important development in U.S.-Costa Rican relations in the early going of the Calderón administration was a new concern over narcotics trafficking. With the end of the East-West ideological struggle, the regional war on communism gave way to a new war on drugs, reflected in renewed U.S. funding to beef up Costa Rican security forces. During the latter years of Calderón's term, and particularly since Figueres took office, relations between Costa Rica and its powerful northern neighbor have maintained a low profile. It was not until October 1994, twenty months after the embassy post had been vacated, that a new U.S. ambassador entered the country.

Nonetheless, the traditional harmony between Costa Rica and the United States has ruptured on several recent occasions. The AFL-CIO brought suit in a U.S. court against the Costa Rican government for its failure to comply with international labor laws. The dispute threatened to repeal Costa Rica's preferential trading status with the United States under the Caribbean Basin Initiative (CBI) and the Generalized System of Preferences (GSP).

Perhaps the most conflictive moment in recent U.S.-Costa Rica relations, however, took place in the months before the 1994 election for general secretary of the Organization of American States (OAS). Costa Ricans expected their Foreign Relations minister Bernd Niehaus to win the post after his considerable efforts to lobby OAS representatives for support. In a surprising turn of events, however, the United States declared its opposition to Niehaus and backed César Gaviria, then president of Colombia. Niehaus characterized the standoff as a confrontation between wealthy countries led by the United States, and small, poor countries, coerced by the northern superpower. Niehaus' eventual defeat was interpreted by Costa Ricans as an attenuation of the traditionally tight bond between Washington and the Costa Rican state.

Like his predecessor, President Figueres revealed his intent to frame foreign policy around foreign trade strategy by naming Fernando Naranjo, nationally renowned economist and previous treasury minister, as his minister of foreign relations. Figueres has distinguished himself from Calderón, however, by demanding that the commercial focus be tempered by some sense of social principle. In his speech at the United Nations forum in October of 1994, Figueres argued for the elimination of the commercial blockade against Cuba and the removal of Haiti's military. Similarly, he sought to restore dynamism to Costa Rica's foreign relations by seizing the regional leadership role on issues of the environment and sustainable development. In contrast to Calderón, Figueres is more committed to cooperative action among the Central American countries.

Security Forces and Crime

Soon after the 1948 civil war José Figueres abolished the army, bringing himself lasting distinction and giving Costa Rica its reputation as the "Switzerland of Central America." The decision to eliminate the military was not "immaculately conceived," as Philip Berryman of the American Friends Service Committee noted. Rather it came at the end of a war fought against a political coalition that had introduced the country's first social reforms. Figueres, who later would adopt and broaden the reforms first instituted by the Calderón government, abolished the army to eliminate a potential threat to the victorious National Liberation movement.

Four decades later Costa Rica still does not have an army, but it does count on a growing police force, much of which has received some military training. At least ten different police agencies now exist. Under the supervision of the Ministry of Justice is the police force of the Office of Judicial Investigation (OIJ), while the Ministry of Public Security administers the Intelligence and Security Department (DIS), the Civil Guard (GC), the Metropolitan Police, Crime Prevention Unit (UPD), and the Office of Drug Control. The Ministry of Government controls the Rural Assistance Guard (GAR) and the immigration police, while traffic police answer to the Ministry of Transportation and Public Works. The Special Support Police (PEA), under the Ministry of Public Security, is the most recently created force. The Immediate Action Unit (UAI), a SWAT-like team known for its Rambo style, was eliminated after an operation in which it killed an innocent young man.

Unlike most other Central American countries, where police and military come under a central command structure, each government ministry in Costa Rica controls its own respective security force. The absence of a common command structure has hindered the security forces from asserting more influence in Costa Rican society, while at the same time rendering them less accountable to public management. Additionally, the persistence of the patronage system causes continuity problems within the security forces. With the exception of the top officers, members of the main security forces are dismissed when a new political party takes over government. For many years politicians have promised the stabilization and professionalization of the police corps, but the distribution of positions within the police continues to be a resource that neither party wishes to lose.

While other government agencies are shrinking, ministries with police forces have experienced steady budget increases. In addition to larger tax allocations, Costa Rican security forces garner international aid from such countries as the United States, South Korea, and Taiwan for externally initiated military training and supplies, counterterrorism assistance, narcotics programs, and monitoring equipment. Along with the health and education ministries, the Ministry of Security has been sheltered in pacts with international financing organizations from the elimination of offices and the layoff of public employees.

Throughout the 1980s, the problems of national security revolved around the Central American conflict. The police corps was trained to confront an armed conflict on the Nicaraguan border, originally in collaboration with the Nicaraguan contras. As the peace process gained hold, however, they sought to impede the contras in their occupation of Costa Rican territory. Police activity also focused on thwarting the "enemies to democracy" through antiterrorist, antisubversive programs against communists, socialists, labor leaders and other leftist groups. Not only did the number of police double during this period but for the first time new security forces were added. In an attempt to slow militarization, President Arias replaced the military-type ranking system within the police corps with titles of Police Colonel, Officer, etc. The Calderón administration reversed this decision, claiming that military ranking bolstered authority and discipline within the security forces.

The contras and their CIA-created support network left behind a legacy of drug smuggling and gun running, while at the same time contributing to the increasing militarization of Costa Rica's police forces. A 1990 report by the U.S. Drug Enforcement Administration (DEA) estimated that at least a ton of cocaine passed through the country each month, while a thousand tons of marijuana are produced annually in Costa Rica. Following the U.S. invasion of Panama, Costa Rica became a favored spot for drug traffickers to launder money. Deregulation of foreign investment and the increased emphasis by recent administrations on exportation have opened up channels for the movement of narcotics and the laundering of money from drug sales.

Under the influence of U.S. foreign policy priorities in the region, the Costa Rican government in the early 1990s identified "El Narcotráfico" as the number one threat to public security. The Legislative

Assembly organized commissions to investigate drug commerce and money laundering networks and passed legislation to check the sale and use of illegal narcotics. The security forces created antiterrorist squads like the Special Intervention Unit (UEI) to collaborate with the U.S. Drug Enforcement Administration (DEA) and the U.S. Information Service (USIS). The United States also contributed funding to train and equip bank functionaries, police officials, and antinarcotics police—including dozens of Costa Rican drug agents who were trained by the Green Berets in Ft. Bragg, North Carolina—to recognize and respond to drug-related activity. One of the most novel developments resulting from bilateral antinarcotics policy is the Anti-Drugs Central Intelligence Group (CICAD) that operates a national radar system for intelligence purposes.

Prior to the build-up of antinarcotics capabilities, drug traffic carried on with virtual impunity from legal enforcement or prosecution. Many of the narcotics-related criminals enjoyed close connections within business and political arenas. In October of 1994, however, the DEA dealt organized crime a major blow when it uncovered the Costa Rican links to an international ring of money launderers. Touting the accomplishments of the operation, which spanned some twenty different countries in the hemisphere, the popular press dubbed Costa Rica the "money laundering capital of Central America."

In addition to drugs, the recent electoral campaign and public opinion polls have indicated that Costa Ricans are increasingly disturbed by an alarming growth in crime and violence in their communities. A well-organized network of car thieves, equipped with sophisticated technology, is responsible for a rash of auto thefts reported throughout the country. Organized gangs of youth, called *chapulines*, roam San José streets assaulting passers-by. In diverse incidents over the course of 1993, Nicaraguan embassy officials, magistrates of the Costa Rican Supreme Court, and the Minister of the Interior were all targets of kidnappings. Not surprisingly gun and home security stores are doing a booming business. And it is becoming increasingly hard to find urban houses that are not fortified with *rejas*, the cast-iron fencework that cages off windows and doors.

Faced with rising crime and violence, many affluent Costa Ricans are opting to protect their lives and property with groups of strongly armed and militarily trained private guards. According to the minister of public security, the number of watchguard organizations operating throughout the country has expanded alarmingly. The trend is particularly significant given that private security teams carry out the functions of state security forces, but without the state's endorsement, and thus are of questionable legality. Private guards are often employed by landlords to dissuade squatters from permanently occupying their land.

The Costa Rican police authorities are hampered in their ability to control violence and crime not only by the magnitude of these problems but also by the fact that they do not enjoy the total confidence of the citizenry. Accusations of police involvement in incidents of robbery, extortion, rape, kidnapping, intimidation and abuse grow yearly. Police have been tied to the illegal trafficking of cattle, the penetration of drugs into the central penitentiaries, and the personal and commercial use of confiscated narcotics. In 1994 agents of the Office of Judicial Investigation (OIJ) were arrested for the torture and execution of famed drug trafficker Ciro Monge. A few years earlier, ten officers from Command Cobra, an antidrug operation in the indigenous zone of Talamanca, were imprisoned for torturing and killing two men, raping several women and terrorizing entire communities. Finally, several OIJ agents were also arrested for murdering a *chapuline* in retribution for the knife wounds he inflicted on an officer who tried to detain him after a mugging in San José.

Unlike elsewhere in Central America, where death squads and paramilitary organizations have terrorized vulnerable citizens, the police forces are the source of many human rights violations in Costa Rica. The police justify their abuses as necessary to maintain order and protect national security. When queried about the excessive number of arbitrary detentions instigated by his office, for example, the director of the Security and Intelligence Department (DIS) replied they were necessary "to intimidate those 'bad' Costa Ricans who have been sniffed out." Many observers speculate that the brutal and indiscriminate behavior results from the military training that police have received since the 1980s.

In March of 1994 the Costa Rican government presented a report to the United Nations Commission on Human Rights concerning Costa Rica's fulfillment of the "Political and Civil Rights Pact." Although the commission approved the report, it expressed concern that several crucial issues were left unexamined. Foremost among these were the prolonged periods of detention endured by individuals who are awaiting court audience, the inadequacy of human rights training received by security forces, and the fact that many labor decrees, particularly those relating to the freedom to organize, do not meet international standards. The UN commission also underscored the preeminent position enjoyed by the Roman Catholic Church in public matters and the fact that certain legal orders enable the National Episcopal Conference to regulate the teaching of religious diversity in the public schools. The commission also concluded that most laws which have been put into place to promote equality among the sexes have not been adequately enforced.

Part 2

Economy

© Donna DeCesare/Impact Visuals

A New Model of Development

Costa Rica's development bubble burst in 1980, when the government suddenly found that it was technically bankrupt and in the midst of the worst recession in its history. The crisis was brought on by the rising interest rates the country found itself paying on its external debt—then the highest per capita debt in Latin America, most of which was owed to private U.S. banks. The context for the financial crisis, however, was the country's development model: an agroexport economy dependent on a few traditional crops, a protected and import-dependent industrial sector, and a benefactor state based on borrowed money. Rising oil prices, a sharp decline in the world price of coffee, and increasingly unfavorable terms of trade brought Costa Rica to the brink of collapse.

As one of the world's least impoverished third world countries, Costa Rica was not a favored recipient of foreign development aid from institutions like the U.S. Agency for International Development (AID) and the World Bank. Neither had it received the emergency attention of the International Monetary Fund (IMF). Suddenly, Costa Rica became the focus of international financial concern. For one thing, foreign donors wanted to avoid the precedent of a third world country stopping interest payments on its debt—which Costa Rica did temporarily in 1981. Another concern, purely political, was the importance to the capitalist world, particularly the United States, that this southern neighbor of revolutionary Nicaragua maintain its economic and political stability. It was deemed essential to keep in good working form this prime example of capitalist democracy in Central America.

The 1980s, then, marked the beginning of a new era in Costa Rica's political and economic development. In 1985 a PLN-led government received the country's first Structural Adjustment Loan (SAL I) extended by the World Bank to downsize the public sector, stimulate private investment, increase nontraditional exports, and reduce tariff rates. Economic liberalization and government reform were a decided shift from the country's roots in the benefactor state and traditional agroexport industry. A second loan (SAL II) was disbursed in 1989 with additional emphases on reducing Costa Rica's budget deficit and the rate of inflation.

By the time the PLN handed over power to the PUSC in 1990, structural reforms seemed to have made a positive impact: the country was enjoying 5 percent growth in gross domestic income, inflation was down to 9 percent, and unemployment stood at 4 percent. In assuming the reins of government, however, the new administration discovered other, less auspicious statistics. During the last year of PLN rule the budget deficit had swelled dangerously—projected to rise to $250 million by the end of 1990. Economic aid from Washington was down about $30 million, and further disbursements of the SAL II were endangered by the climbing budget deficit, which was nearly twice the ceiling previously set by the World Bank. Inflation was expected to increase sharply as a result of an across-the-board 15 percent increase in the price of gasoline and the rates of the state-owned water, telephone, and electric company.

Upon taking office, Calderón warned Costa Ricans that they should prepare for two tough years of austerity measures to resolve what he described as "the worst fiscal crisis in the country's history."[1] It was expected that Calderón, despite his populist pretensions, would follow the neoliberal economic policies of the PLN administrations. The appointment of Jorge Guardia, a harsh critic of the PLN's gradualistic approach to structural adjustment, to head the Central Bank indicated that the pace of this conservative economic adjustment program would pick up during the Calderón government.

In January of 1994, one month before the national elections, the Calderón administration boasted of achieving a national growth rate of over 6 percent during its final two years in office. In Calderón's disfavor, however, the foreign trade deficit had magnified to $844 million. When the PLN took over in May, Figueres discovered that the

Figure 2a

Costa Rica's External Debt

External Debt (1993)	$3.96 billion
Debt Service Actually Paid (1993)	$588 million
Outstanding External Debt as % of GDP (1992)	52%
Debt Service as % of exports (1992)	20%

SOURCES: Inter-American Development Bank (IDB), 1994; AID, 1994.

fiscal deficit projected for 1994 approached 7 percent of national production. In the ensuing months, the government raised the price of fuel and electricity, deregulated prices for basic foodstuffs (sugar, bread, milk, etc.), and announced plans to reduce public spending and impose a new tax regimen (Figure 2a).

Entering 1995 Costa Rica's rate of inflation had climbed to nearly twenty percent—4 points higher than the government's goal.[2] Provoked in part by the government bailout of the Anglo Costarricense Bank, the state's fiscal dilemma pressured Figueres to accept a third round of structural adjustment loans (SAL III). Costa Rica would receive $350 million in loans from the World Bank and Inter-American Development Bank, but 8,000 workers would have to be cut over a four-year period from the public payroll. Assistance plans were further complicated when World Bank officials tied the release of their $100 million share of SAL III to a full accord between Costa Rica and the IMF. Negotiations with the IMF had fallen through after the Figueres administration failed to convince the multilateral lending agency that it was taking the necessary steps to reduce the fiscal deficit. By March a new agreement was in the works to cut public spending and restore Costa Rica to the IMF's good graces.

Privatization of the State

Since the 1940s the public sector has stood at the center of Costa Rica's political and economic development. By the early 1980s one out of every five working Costa Ricans was employed by the state.[3] Though costly, public services have contributed to the high quality of life in the country. Government insurance, health care, and social security services have made Costa Rica one of the healthiest nations in the third world. Free access to public education has elevated the rate of literacy to 93 percent of the population. The state electric company produces most of Costa Rica's electricity from hydropower, and the government-owned telephone company is responsible for a highly automated and efficient system that reaches 80 percent of the population.[4]

But the economic crisis that gripped the nation in 1980 forced a radical cost/benefit evaluation of many state institutions. Blame for the country's economic difficulties was placed, in large part, on the public sector, which the neoliberal adjusters accused of distorting the economy with its intervention. Under the programs of structural adjustment, austerity measures and privatization were proposed as the remedies.

In response, the state embarked on a program to reduce government employment and public salary increases, trim the social services budget, and reorganize the public pension system. The most visible privatizing effort involved opening up the financial sector to private banks. Foreign lending institutions would like to dismantle completely the nationalized banking system, which the PLN set in place in 1949 to expand credit opportunities for all economic classes. Few in Costa Rica are ready for such a frontal attack on what has been a centerpiece of their society. Nonetheless, the ongoing financial restructuring is steadily eating away at the government banking system and each year places more funds in the coffers of new, private financial institutions. It is likely that the Anglo Costarricense Bank scandal of 1994 will lend force to this trend.

Selling off state corporations is another facet of privatization. Under a plan financed by AID, the subsidiaries of CODESA, the state development corporation, are being sold. Other public sector institutions have also been threatened with privatization, including the National Production Council (CNP) and the Costa Rican Electricity Institute (ICE).

The third aspect of privatization affects various state service agencies, ranging from road construction and low-income housing departments to the laundry service at state hospitals. Clinics, birth control services, and agricultural assistance are also being shed by the state and in some cases offered to corporations or cooperatives established by former public sector employees at government prompting.

Privatization must certainly be considered as part of the solution to Costa Rica's enduring budget deficits. In the late 1980s, however, privatization came to be regarded not simply as one possible remedy but as part of an all-encompassing ideological imperative. Even the most lucrative of state enterprises were targeted for change: the National Institute of Insurance (INS), the Costa Rican Petroleum Refinery (RECOPE), and the National Liquor Factory (FANAL). Advocates of reform argued that the state's involvement in corporate affairs made a mockery of free market principles. Still, there is enduring resistance to the notion of privatizing all state industries, many of which have long formed a kind of petty cash box for central government.

As privatization continues, its uneven nature has become clear. Designated for radical surgery are only those areas of government that are considered unproductive—meaning that they do not contribute directly to economic growth and the creation of foreign exchange. In contrast, special treatment is accorded to that part of the state which (with the blessings and funding of foreign donors) orients services to the private sector, particularly those businesses that produce for export.

An array of government services and financial rewards are directed to new investors, and the government is spending more money on the export-promotion services of CENPRO (Export Promotion Center) and on the creation of export-processing free zones—all the while cutting back the budget of state institutions that benefit the broader Costa Rican society. CEPAS, a social and economic research center in San José, concluded that privatization "is not simply the dismantling of the state, but the redefinition of its functions." Ironically, many of the strongest advocates of a "minimal state" benefit from government business incentives or luxurious state pensions.

The privatization of state functions has proceeded slowly. Costa Ricans derive a certain sense of security from the services offered by the state, as well as pride for some of its stellar institutions. Despite the resentment that many occasionally experience over inefficient bureaucracy, the voracity that private enterprise has shown for state operations is a constant reminder that privatization could eventually swallow up access to even the most basic of services. Reacting to the neoliberal tide that recently swept through government, the Figueres administration voiced an intent to displace the "minimal state" ideology that has come to dominate discourse on state reform. Rather than privatization, it argued that what is needed is a thorough housecleaning aimed at making state services more efficient and more responsive to public needs.[5]

Back to the Export Model

Government austerity and privatization constitute only one side of structural adjustment. An equally dramatic revamping of the country's productive sectors is also under way. In the 1980s, renewed attention was placed on the diversification of production for export. In accordance with the economics of comparative advantage, the IMF, AID, and the World Bank all insisted that there be an increased effort to promote exports that are competitively priced in the world market. Such items included labor-intensive textiles or electronic goods in the industrial sector and vegetables, flowers, and other nontraditional crops in the agricultural sector. Export fever, which has spread from foreign lending agencies to the government and business elite, was promoted in Costa Rica with the slogan "Exportar es Bueno" (It's Good to Export).

The process of structural adjustment has been a gradual one in which the social pact with the poor and the working class has not been entirely abandoned. Weighing neoliberal reforms against electoral pressures, the PLN and PUSC alike have fought off demands from international financial institutions for even harsher austerity

Figure 2b

Costa Rica's GDP by Economic Sector: 1950, 1992

1950

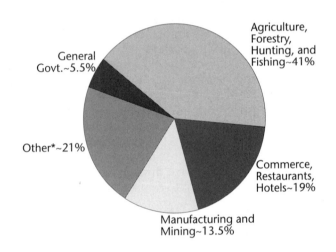

General Govt.~5.5%

Agriculture, Forestry, Hunting, and Fishing~41%

Other*~21%

Commerce, Restaurants, Hotels~19%

Manufacturing and Mining~13.5%

1992

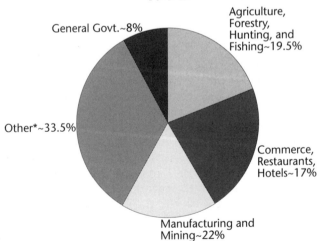

General Govt.~8%

Agriculture, Forestry, Hunting, and Fishing~19.5%

Other*~33.5%

Commerce, Restaurants, Hotels~17%

Manufacturing and Mining~22%

SOURCES: Costa Rica Ministry of Planning and Economic Policy (MIDEPLAN), United Nations Development Program (UNDP), *Costa Rica en Cifras: 1950-1992*, 1994.

*Electricity and water; construction; transportation; storage; communications; insurance and financial services, real estate, and other personal services.

measures and a more complete privatization program. This has led some policy analysts to comment on the "heterodoxical" character of Costa Rica's structural adjustment, which has balanced market reforms and fiscal conservatism with continuing protections and services for the working class and the poor. The government, for example, decided to cut back public employment on a voluntary rather than mandatory basis. The government has also negotiated with international finance organizations to exclude health, education, and security sectors from the wave of government layoffs. In addition, the state also provides credit through government-owned banks to enable workers and social organizations to acquire state corporations. The PLN has dubbed this tempered approach to political and economic reform as "Structural Adjustment ' Tico' style."

The Organization of Production

In the last forty years Costa Rica's rural areas have seen profound transformation. Through the 1950s, agriculture formed the country's heart and soul, absorbing nearly 50 percent of the national labor force and composing 95 percent of its exports. Coffee and bananas were the primary products and the few existing industries were small, rudimentary, and oriented towards domestic consumption.

Following World War II, rising world prices for raw materials and agricultural products prompted Costa Rica to expand its export offerings to include sugar cane and beef. In the wake of these changes, programs to promote export production came to dominate agricultural policy, leaving the cultivation of basic foodstuffs for internal consumption in the hands of small farmers, with deficits in production being covered by imports.[6] At the same time, the government launched a program of import-substitution industrialization that, unlike agricultural policy, aimed to increase production for domestic and regional markets. Costa Rica's incorporation into the Central American Common Market, the state's increasing involvement in economic development, and the urbanization of the Central Valley all contributed to industrial development.

Between 1950 and 1992 the dominant patterns of production in Costa Rica changed considerably (Figure 2b). Industry's contribution to the Gross Domestic Product jumped to 22 percent, up from 13 percent in 1950.[7] Despite the expansion of export production and growth of the banana and coffee export sectors, agriculture's role in national production fell precipitously. By 1992 less than a quarter of the labor force worked in the agricultural sector, while industry absorbed 18 percent. Largely due to urbanization and the expansion of the state, the service sector—including such activities as commerce, transport, and construction—had also achieved a central place in national production and work-force participation (Figure 2c).

Agriculture

In response to the economic crisis that plagued the country in the 1980s, Costa Rican agriculture underwent an overhaul aimed at making local food production more efficient while increasing agroexports. This sectoral adjustment, which the government called its "Changing Agriculture" policy, was imposed by international lending institutions with the consent and approval of the Monge and Arias governments.

The "Changing Agriculture" policy attempted to rectify two weaknesses of Costa Rican agriculture: 1) its overdependence on a few traditional agroexports, namely coffee and bananas, and 2) the perceived

Figure 2c
Employment by Economic Sector, 1993

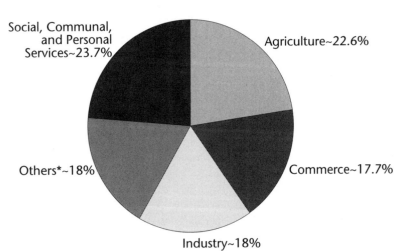

SOURCE: Costa Rica Ministry of Economy, Industry, and Commerce, General Office of Statistics and Censuses, 1993.
*Electricity, gas, and water; construction; transportation; storage and communications; financial establishments.

inefficiency and backwardness of the local food-producing sector. The government addressed these concerns from the perspective of free market and comparative advantage economics, which is to say that it promoted agricultural production that was competitive in the international market while reducing its support for nonexport crops (Figure 2d).

Encouraged and financed by both the government and international financial institutions, nontraditional agroexport production intensified in the 1980s. For most Costa Rican small-scale farmers, however, this new emphasis represented a challenge to their very existence, in part, because it took such issues as commodity prices and quality standards out of their hands. Foreign-controlled export houses and traders decide how much and what standard of products to accept, often leaving bewildered farmers stuck with unmarketable produce. In the early 1980s the World Bank promoted cocoa production among small farmers, but then world market prices took a nose-

Figure 2d
Costa Rica's Structure of Agrarian Production

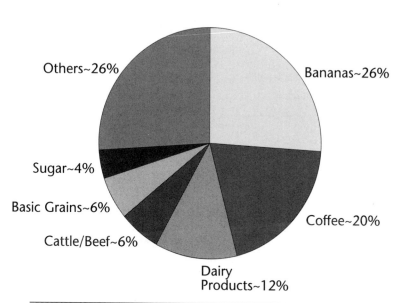

Others~26% Bananas~26%

Sugar~4%

Basic Grains~6%

Cattle/Beef~6%

Coffee~20%

Dairy Products~12%

SOURCE: Secretary of Planning for the Agricultural Sector (SEPSA), *Diagnóstico del Sector Agropecuario*, 1993.

dive, leaving many farmers with large debts and no market for their nontraditional produce.[8] The stress on export crops also directed credit and technical assistance away from small farmers and to the large commercial-level operations that had easier access to foreign markets.

The result was turmoil and conflict in rural Costa Rica as basic grain farmers discovered they no longer had access to government credit and price guarantees. Unable to produce profitably under these conditions, these producers failed to plant enough beans, corn, and rice to feed the nation. The resulting food deficits were met with increased grain imports, some channeled through U.S. food aid programs. Many small-scale producers have been forced to sell their lands because they receive virtually no incentives for grain production and face the difficulties of adapting to the "new agriculture."

In the last few electoral campaigns, presidential candidates have been confronted with a series of demands from small farmers and campesinos—a sector many regard as the keystone of Costa Rican democracy. But the chronic budget deficit and the restrictions imposed by international financial institutions make new government funds hard to come by. There is also a question about the sincerity of such campaign promises. Given the government's deepening commitment to agribusiness and agroexport production, it is unlikely that the government will make a concerted effort to resolve the plight of the small farmer. In an era when export production is seen as the remedy to virtually all the country's political and economic maladies, the family farming sector is viewed as a backward element of the economy that has no role in the modern marketplace. Nevertheless, the campesino is never totally abandoned. During the Calderón administration, nearly 25,000 new land titles were distributed to rural dwellers— nearly 40 percent of all titles that the state has ever authorized. Figueres, for his part, has initiated an expansive credit program for the small producer.

Industry

Costa Rica's industrial sector developed in the 1960s mostly as a result of the Central American Common Market, which gave manufacturers a larger market for their goods. The country has two general categories of industrial investment: one which produces primarily for local or regional markets and another that simply uses Costa Rica as an export platform for textile and electronic goods produced with low-cost, unorganized labor.

The first class of investment has benefited from what are known as import substitution tariff protections, which afford businesses a sheltered market to produce and sell their goods. This industrial sector is resisting structural adjustment measures that threaten the protected status of import substitution industry. It calls for a slower pace of adjustment and for low-interest, government-guaranteed loans to help make local industry more competitive both regionally and internationally. Export-oriented investment also benefits from government incentive and tax exemption provisions designed to attract foreign companies to the country.

Food processing, beverage, and tobacco companies—many of which are controlled by U.S. transnational corporations—form the fastest growing sectors of Costa Rica's manufacturing industry. Combined with the manufacture of chemicals, rubber, plastics, and machinery, they represent almost 80 percent of national industrial production (Figure 2e).

Industrial activities are principally directed toward internal markets: 78 percent of production is consumed domestically and about 22

Figure 2e
Costa Rica's Structure of Industrial Production

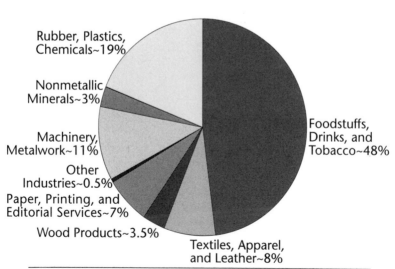

Rubber, Plastics, Chemicals~19%

Nonmetallic Minerals~3%

Machinery, Metalwork~11%

Other Industries~0.5%

Paper, Printing, and Editorial Services~7%

Wood Products~3.5%

Foodstuffs, Drinks, and Tobacco~48%

Textiles, Apparel, and Leather~8%

SOURCE: Costa Rica Chamber of Industries, *Principales Indicadores*, June 1994

percent is exported. This trend is not uniform across industries, however; while textiles, rubber and clothing companies export from 50 to 75 percent of their production, 75 to 100 percent of foodstuffs, drinks, tobacco, and furniture are both manufactured and consumed in Costa Rica.[9]

Industrial activity, which is strongly concentrated in San José, is characterized by a few large and many small and medium-sized enterprises. Ninety percent of industrial establishments employ fewer than fifty workers, and only 6 percent have more than 100 employees. Seventy two percent of Costa Rican workers are salaried (20 percent work independently and 16 percent are employed by the public sector). Measured by size of labor force, food and clothing form the most important sectors of the manufacturing economy.

Exports

Since 1983, a boom in nontraditional exports and foreign investment has led to characterizations of Costa Rica as "one of the third world's most successful cases of transition toward an export-led growth strategy in the 1980s."[10] Principal factors promoting the expansion of exports include: an economic policy developed in the 1980s that explicitly aims to boost export production by offering valuable incentives to exporters; trade agreements like the Caribbean Basin Initiative (CBI) that make U.S. markets more accessible to Costa Rican products; and the AID-backed creation of private organizations like the Coalition of Initiatives for Development (CINDE) and the Investment Promotion Program (PIE) to seek out markets, commercial contacts, and foreign investment opportunities for export production. The value of Costa Rican exports in 1983 was nearly $87 million; ten years later, in 1993, the value of exports had leapt to more than $2 billion. Under "Plan 2000," the government aspires to increase exports to $5 billion by the turn of the century.

The overall success of Costa Rica's export sector can be attributed to the promotion of nontraditional goods, which forms a principal condition of the country's structural adjustment loan agreements with the World Bank. According to the most common definition a "nontraditional export" includes: a) a product that is being produced and exported for the very first time or b) a product that was traditionally produced for the local or regional market and that now is sent to a tertiary market outside the region. In the particular case of Costa Rica, coffee, bananas, sugar, and beef are considered traditional and all other products nontraditionals. This includes the industrial sector for which *all* exports are considered nontraditionals, even when they were previously produced in the country or were being sold in Central American markets (which do not constitute tertiary markets). Between 1990 and 1993 nontraditional goods increased from 51 to 57 percent of all exports, while traditional products decreased from 49 to 43 percent.[11]

The government has pursued three primary strategies to attract foreign investment and promote nontraditional export production: export contracts, free trade zones, and temporary admissions (*maquilas*). Government-offered export contracts enable corporations to escape taxes and tariffs on production inputs, export sales, and profits. The government also offers tax reductions on the repatriation of profits from export operations and guarantees an investor's right to transfer profits. The most inviting incentive extended by these agreements, however, involves the Tributary Savings Certificates (CATs). Negotiable on the country's stock market, CATs amount to 15 percent of a company's nontraditional exports when their domestic value-added is greater than 35 percent.

Tributary Savings Certificates have cost the state dearly. In 1989, CATs added up to 6 percent of the national budget and, if estimates from 1991 are any judge, CAT costs account for nearly 60 percent of the fiscal deficit.[12] Moreover, a World Bank study demonstrated that, given the extensive use of imports in the production of nontraditional exports, approximately half of the costs in CATs are used to pay for imported goods.[13] Also noteworthy is the finding that CATs tend to concentrate in the hands of a small group of large companies.[14] PINDECO, a pineapple export company subsidiary to Del Monte, cashed in on nearly 10 percent of the value of all CATs granted during a period of 18 months. In 1992, after almost five years of negotiations, the World Bank, the International Monetary Fund, and various domestic sectors succeeded in eliminating the concession of further tax certificates. They argued that CATs constituted an excessive burden on the state and an unjustified benefit for corporate enterprise.

The development of free trade zones (FTZs) is another government strategy to stimulate export production. Like all companies that export, those situated in the industrial parks created by FTZs benefit from tax exemptions on imports, land, sales, purchases, profits, and capital transfers. Industries that take greatest advantage of the free trade zones include textiles, electronics, and agroindustry.[15] In 1993, 134 companies operated in Costa Rica's eight free trade zones, up from eleven in 1986.[16]

A free trade zone—a type of enclave economy—generally benefits the state only through the generation of employment. In 1986, FTZs employed around 2,500 workers, in 1992, 13,608 workers, and by 1993, the free trade zone work force had risen to 18,581. Often touted as the solution to unemployment and poverty, free trade zone companies receive additional benefits if they locate in the most depressed zones of the country, particularly the port towns.

The Temporary Admissions or Maquila Program, extends the same benefits as free trade zones but with the important exception that *maquiladoras* can set up independently almost anywhere in the country. In addition to the machinery they import, *maquiladoras* bring in partially manufactured goods that they assemble for re-export. In 1992 textile production accounted for 70 percent of Costa Rica's *maquila* companies and generated 90 percent of *maquila* exports. Electronics, mechanical parts, prosthetics and food products are other important *maquila* industries. Nearly 90 percent of *maquila* exports go to the United States and 5 percent to Taiwan.[17]

Without a doubt, the vast majority of foreign companies that come to Costa Rica are drawn by the promise of cheap manual labor and by the unrestricted movement of capital and goods. Free Trade Zones and the *maquila* industry exact a high price in the form of tax write-offs on corporate profits. Advocates of free trade zone development extol the benefits of employment generation and labor training; but jobs typically are low paying, highly unstable and routinized, requiring few skills. *Maquiladoras* and FTZ enterprises make a specific point of hiring women for assembly line jobs because they accept lower wages and are held to be more readily disciplined than men. Although *maquila* and FTZ exports are an important source of foreign earnings, these industries create few, if any, links with other sectors of the Costa Rican economy. Most of their production inputs come from outside the country.

Technically considered an export, Costa Rica's tourist industry has also experienced considerable growth in recent years. Indeed, by 1993 it had become the second most important source of foreign currency behind banana exports—prompting some to exuberantly label it a "21st century gold nugget." Between 1983 and 1992, the number of tourists visiting the country almost doubled, to more than 600,000. Given recent reductions in export quotas for bananas by the European Union (EU), many predict tourism will soon become the top generator of foreign earnings (Figure 2f).

Despite the considerable gains made in industrial development in the last decade, agricultural production continues to provide the source of most of Costa Rica's exports. In 1992 agricultural goods constituted 52 percent of total foreign trade while the manufacturing industry accounted for 46 percent of export earnings. Although traditional products—including coffee, bananas, meat, and sugar— have demonstrated only slow growth, in 1993 they still represented about two-thirds of the total value of agricultural exports. The two leading agroexports, coffee and bananas, are shipped primarily to the United States and the EU.

Bananas

Costa Rica is the world's second highest exporter of bananas, following Ecuador. In 1993 exports of this fruit constituted the country's largest source of foreign earnings, representing 50 percent of all agricultural trade abroad.

In spite of a dramatic decline in banana production that followed the 1984 announcement by United Brands that it was terminating its

Figure 2f

Costa Rica's Principal Exports and Imports

In millions of U.S. $

Exports, 1994

Bananas	537
Tourism	505
Coffee	203
Maquilas	116
Free Trade Zones	103
Meat	67
Shrimp	57
Pineapples	54
Women's Apparel	46
Medicines	45
Fish	34
Ornamental Plants	34
Fish Preservatives	31
Decorative Plant Parts	30
Sugar	29
Rubber Packing	28
Total	$1,919

Imports, 1993

Raw Materials	1,059
Consumer Goods	822
Capital Goods	721
Construction Materials	93
Fuel and Lubricants	174
Total	$2,869

SOURCE: Center for the Promotion of Exports and Investments (CENPRO), 1994; Economist Intelligence Unit, *EIU Country Report: Costa Rica*, 1995.

banana business in Costa Rica, banana exports have been on the rebound since 1988. Renewed growth parallels an increase in banana activity worldwide and can be attributed to the government's Banana Promotion Plan that has expanded the acreage devoted to banana production. Between 1988 and 1993 land under banana cultivation more than doubled, aided in part by the appearance of three new agroindustrial companies: Geest Caribbean, Difrusa, and Nobility.

Banana production is characterized by the enclave structure of a plantation economy in that there are few ties with other economic sectors. The banana companies exploit local labor and resources but otherwise contribute little to regional development. Foreign corporations, led by RJ Reynolds (Del Monte/BANDECO) and Castle & Cooke (Standard Fruit/Dole), dominate the industry. Local growers account for about 50 percent of production, but foreign companies control packaging and export stages, including around 90 percent of the total volume of banana exports. In 1993 Costa Rican bananas were shipped primarily to the United States (53 percent), West Germany (19 percent), Belgium (19 percent) and Italy (7 percent).[18] In response to banana import quotas imposed by the EU, Costa Rica is seeking new outlets in Eastern Europe and Southeast Asia.

Plantation laborers have filed numerous denunciations against banana companies for their refusal to abide by labor norms, for deforesting vast tracts of land, and for polluting rivers and soil with agrochemicals. Pesticide use in banana production has been blamed for widespread sterility among banana workers and deformities among children born in banana production zones.[19] In combination with an agricultural policy that offers few incentives to basic grain production, banana expansion has obliged many small farmers to sell their land and seek work on banana plantations.

The Banana Unions Network has pursued aggressive lobbying tactics, even to the point of supporting EU quotas, to limit banana expansion and make companies accountable for their labor practices. Its initiatives have won it the censure of political and business figures, many of whom regard the banana industry not as a lucrative business venture for a few wealthy capitalists but as an activity of critical national interest. The Unions Network is severely hampered in its advocacy efforts by the constant threat of worker layoffs in regions where plantation labor forms the primary source of employment.

Coffee

Revenues from Costa Rica's second most voluminous agroexport, coffee, are buffeted by constant fluctuations in international prices and quotas. The country is favored, however, by its high quality coffee and ideal growing conditions. An estimated 130,000 farmers cultivate coffee in Costa Rica, most in the form of small and medium-sized operations that sell to large processing plants and export warehouses. Historians and sociologists point to the relatively uniform distribution of land that characterized coffee production throughout history as having laid the foundation for Costa Rican democracy. The state has long regulated relations between exporters and farmers to ensure that the latter are guaranteed a just price for their harvests. At various historic junctures coffee growers have also formed powerful political blocs in defense of their common interests.

In the 1980s foreign investors began to exert greater control over the coffee sector. Liberalized laws allowed foreign traders to finance local exporters and processors, facilitating the purchase of shares in domestic exporting companies and coffee mills. Foreign companies that gained influence during the 1980s include Volkart, Jacobs, Lonrays, and Ruthfos. Together with local investors, Volkart opened the country's most modern coffee mill, Beneficio 2000, in late 1988.

Coffee exports declined during the early 1990s due to a precipitous fall in world prices and efforts by Costa Rican and other Central American exporters to restore the crop's value by deliberately withholding supply. By 1994 the strategy appeared to have succeeded, boding well for coffee. The EU is the largest buyer of coffee beans; in 1993 it bought 62 percent of this crop. The United States follows Germany as the most important national buyer.

Figure 2g

Costa Rican Exports by Region of Destination, 1993

In millions of U.S. $

North America	1,000.0	48%
European Union	500.0	24%
Central America	348.0	17%
Caribbean	78.0	4%
South America	52.0	3%
Asia	46.5	2%
All Others	42.5	2%
Total	$2,067.0	

SOURCE: Center for the Promotion of Exports and Investments (CENPRO), *Sintesis de Exportaciones 1993*, 1994.

Beef and Sugar

Shrinking markets in the United States combined with rising production costs precipitated a severe slump in the beef industry, which emerged about 1970 to meet rising U.S. demand for cheap, lean beef. In response to declining foreign demand, ranchers have reduced their herds, which has resulted domestically in higher prices and decreased consumption. Although local beef consumption is declining, broiler chicken production and consumption have boomed. "Chickenburgers," from poultry fed on imported yellow corn, are sold at the many fast-food outlets in San José.

Since the 1980s, rising international prices and increased U.S. quotas have helped Costa Rica's sugar industry to regain vigor. Virtually all sugar exports, including sugar-based ethanol, go to the United States.

Nontraditionals

Nontraditional exports, industrial as well as agricultural, display rapid growth and form the largest sector of the Costa Rican economy. The principal areas of nontraditional production include pineapple, seafood, textiles, medicines, and decorative plants. Agricultural nontraditionals, consisting primarily of ornamental plants and flowers, roots, tubers and fruit (pineapples, melons, strawberries, and papayas), make up 23 percent of the total value of nontraditional exports. Industrial goods—primarily women's apparel, medicines, seafood preservatives, and rubber packing—compose 70 percent of nontraditional exports.

As Costa Rica's principal external market, the United States draws 48 percent of Costa Rica's traditional and nontraditional exports.[20] The EU receives about a quarter and Central America about 17 percent of Costa Rican sales in the exterior (Figure 2g). Over two-fifths of Costa Rica's imports come from the United States.[21]

In addition to expanding and diversifying export production, a central thrust of Costa Rica's neo-export strategy has been to diversify the market destinations of its products. Regional political and military conflict during the 1980s depressed commerce with Central America, once the country's number two consumer of exports. From 1980 to 1991, Central America's share of Costa Rican industrial exports dropped from 72 to 32 percent.[22] Offsetting this trend, U.S. and Canadian markets have expanded their influence, stimulated by commercial accords like the 1984 Caribbean Basin Initiative (CBI).

Foreign Investment

Accompanying the growth of agricultural exports, aggressive penetration of foreign capital has given rise to the heralded "transnationalization of Costa Rican agriculture." Foreign presence in agroindustry is indeed impressive: Two transnational corporations—British American Tobacco and Philip Morris—control tobacco production and processing. Del Monte controls most pineapple, mango, papaya, chayote, and lemon exports. Including bananas, Del Monte's agroexports represent 9 percent of the country's total export production. United Brands controls palm oil production and exports, as well as the domestic production of margarine and shortening. Approximately 80 percent of fern exports, 50 percent of cut flower production, and 40 percent of macadamia nut exports are controlled by foreign investors.

Foreign capital has also entered the industrial sector, especially through the Temporary Admission and Free Trade Zone programs. In many cases foreign investment takes the form of the purchase of locally owned companies. More than fifty years after its establishment, the chocolate factory "El Gallito" (the Little Rooster), a virtual symbol of Costa Rican nationalism, was acquired by the Philip Morris Company. Another Costa Rican property, Monpik Ice Cream, was recently bought jointly by the Mexican firm Quant Mexico, the Guatemalan firm Helados Mariposa, and Costa Rican associates. CPC International bought the Lizano sauces factory, another national symbol, and acquired the rights to Chiquita Brands and Numar to produce Clover and Hellman's mayonnaise. Foreign transnationals have established their presence in the metals and machinery industries as well.[23]

Another sector that exhibits impressive growth due to transnational investments is tourism. Following a recent boom in tourist trade in Costa Rica, foreign firms have descended upon the capital city and coastal towns with plans for luxury hotels and tourist "megaprojects". Growing interest in tourism is attributed to the international attention Costa Rica derived from ex-president Oscar Arias' winning of the Nobel Peace Prize, as well as publicity surrounding the country's national park system. As the tourist complexes spread, many Costa Ricans feel they are becoming strangers in their own country. Despite encouraging signs, tourist development is also plagued by the ever-present fear that visiting Costa Rica is a fad that will eventually lose its appeal to the fickle international tourism industry.

Costa Ricans have a history of ambivalence toward the growth of foreign investment in their country. Attempts by foreign companies to mine national bauxite reserves in the 1970s met with waves of popular protest. Today foreign investment is regarded as omnipresent and inevitable, and is grudgingly accepted due to the potential for employment generation and technology transfer. Every now and again, one hears the discordant voice of a politician or disgruntled citizen warning against the "sale of the country piece by piece," but for the most part, the nationalist ideals of two decades ago are dismissed as dated and obsolete. The penetration of foreign investors has been aided by associations established between some national leaders and foreign businesses. Former president Rafael Calderón Fournier, for example, was hired on as a lawyer to the private Mexican bank BANCRECEN.

Privatization of the Finance Industry

The dust still has not settled after the government—under pressure from AID, the IMF, and the World Bank—opened the door to private banking in a country where the entire banking system existed under state control for more than three and a half decades. Predictably, a number of private banks opened shop only to bilk depositors of their savings certificates and then collapse. In early 1995 Costa Rica had some twenty private banks in addition to four government institutions. The private banking has been rapidly expanding—at an average annual rate of 91 percent for credit offerings during the 1980s. However, as a result of all the interest in private banking by foreign donors, many private banks are swimming in credit they cannot get rid of. The state banks retain a monopoly on checking and savings accounts although private banks can accept time deposits. The insurance industry, like banking, was also nationalized long ago, but still remains under state control.

In September of 1994 the national banking system lost its oldest and, arguably, most revered institution. The Anglo Costarricense Bank (BAC) closed its doors following losses totaling more than $100 million resulting from speculative investments in Venezuelan debt bonds, the purchase of illegal Panamanian subsidiaries, and careless credit management. Slamming the BAC's former directors, President Figueres lamented: "Irregular acts committed by people without scruples produced the magnitude of the losses—funds with which we could have eliminated all of the country's slums." [24]

Perhaps the most important revelation surrounding the Anglo Bank's fall, however, is that the state banking system has failed to fulfill the social and economic functions for which it was originally conceived. Extremely high spreads between interest rates on loans and deposits, sometimes in excess of 15 points, were necessary to sustain state institutions because of inefficient loan recuperation and elevated costs of operation. As a result, the price of credit rose to nearly 40 percent, diminishing considerably the access to credit by small and microenterprises. This condition underscores the need for financing institutions to be well managed prior to embarking on programs in support of development. Each day the sentiment grows that the people who most benefit from national banks, business people and well-connected family groups, do not justify the banks' existence.

Macroeconomy: "History Repeats Itself"

By the mid-1980s it appeared that Costa Rica had shaken the crisis that seized the country in 1979. Its debt payments were back on track, its exports increased, and it had achieved positive economic growth. Since that time, however, Costa Ricans have become painfully aware of recurring cycles of budget deficits and inflation. The first two years of each four-year administrative term since 1982 (Monge, Arias, Calderón and most recently Figueres) have been marked by new taxes and austerity measures aimed at reducing the deficit and controlling inflation. But in the remaining two years, usually after the economy has achieved some degree of stability, public leaders cast aside their conservative moorings to go on a spending spree aimed at restoring their popularity—thus destabilizing government finances once again. Inevitably, the incoming president declares in his inaugural speech that "the state coffers are empty" and that his first years in office will focus on repairing government finances. Usually this means postponing campaign promises to farmers, labor, and the poor, and seeking new accords with the IMF and World Bank. In this way history repeats itself, revolving from the populism of the electoral campaigns to the neoliberal undertakings of the governing state.

With the echoes of 1994 campaign slogans still ringing in their heads, Costa Ricans already suspect that the newly elected PLN-led government intends to carry on the tradition of revolving government focus. Despite unveiling his new and comprehensive Plan to Combat Poverty, Figueres has devoted his first year in office to outlining measures to control the budget deficit and growing inflation. With Structural Adjustment Program III now gearing up, and new reductions in the state's budget and work force planned for the future, it

Figure 2h

Change in Exports and Imports, 1983-1993

In millions of U.S. $

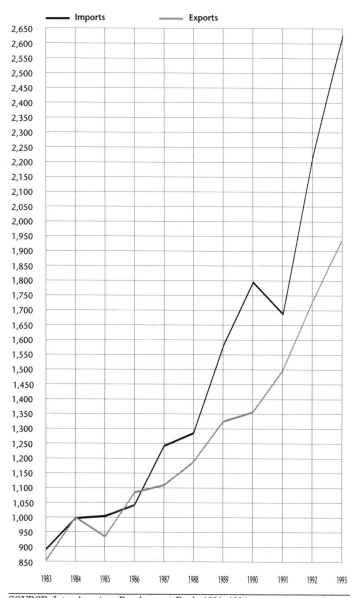

SOURCE: Inter-American Development Bank, 1991, 1994.

seems unlikely that Costa Rica will ever escape the vicious cycle of austerity measures, temporary economic stability and renewed crisis.

In fact, with more than ten years of structural adjustment under its belt, Costa Rica now seems headed for further decline rather than improvement. Despite the explicit aims of state reform and economic liberalization measures, inflation remains uncontrollable and the external debt has grown instead of diminished. Although exports of textiles, pineapples, and other nontraditionals have increased, imports have expanded even more dramatically, magnifying the trade deficit by 600 percent between 1985 and 1990 (Figure 2h).

The signs of social deterioration are even more tangible when viewed from the ground level. Costa Rica's lower and middle-income populations—especially small farmers and wage workers—clearly have borne the greatest burden of structural reform, while the import, nontraditional export, and financial sectors all have prospered. Campesino leaders report a "frightening concentration of land ownership" resulting from the new non-traditional emphasis in agricultural policy that favors corporate agroindustry.[25] From 1980 to 1990 wages dropped nearly 17 percent—despite an overall growth in the GDP (Figure 2i). What more telling indicators are needed to conclude that structural adjustment has widened the gap between rich and poor?

Figure 2i
Change in GDP, 1983-1993

Percentage change from previous year

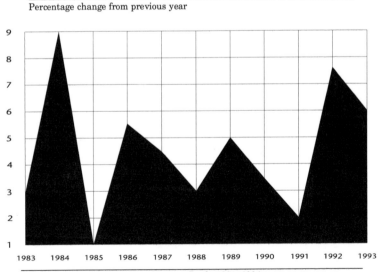

SOURCE: Inter-American Development Bank, 1991, 1994.

Part 3

Social Conditions

© Donna DeCesare/Impact Visuals

Social Policy in the Context of Structural Adjustment

Costa Rica's social indicators began to improve rapidly in the 1950s as the country's economic structure was transformed and the government started to institutionalize its social policy. As Costa Rican sociologist Ana Sojo notes, "It is indisputable that social policy has played a fundamental role in the political stability achieved by Costa Rican society in the second half of the twentieth century." [1]

In the years following the "Revolution of 1948," the government came to view its social and economic development policies as closely intertwined. Improvement of the nation's social welfare was regarded as much more than an automatic product of economic growth. Instead, the well-being of the population was seen as a precondition for economic progress and the responsibility of the government itself. [2]

By the early 1970s, however, it had become evident that the state's strategies were insufficient to the task of adequately improving living conditions in the country, and a new round of social policy changes ensued. In 1970 President José Figueres Ferrer created the Social Assistance Institute (IMAS) as an instrument to combat poverty and extend affordable health care to Costa Ricans of all socioeconomic backgrounds. Acting on this resolve, the government nationalized the nation's hospitals and integrated health care personnel into a national medical system that reached out for the first time to rural areas. Social security health coverage was greatly expanded. With proceeds from new taxes on sales and salaries, the government also created the Family Allowances and Social Development Fund (FODESAF) to provide a self-sustaining source of financing for welfare programs. The early 1970s were also characterized by the state's build-up of work force training programs, public services infrastructure, and programs to construct low-income housing and redistribute land. [3]

Figure 3a

Figure 3a
Distribution of Government Social Services Budget

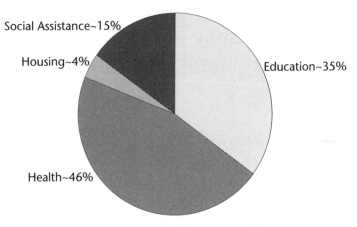

1981

Social Assistance~15%

Housing~4%

Education~35%

Health~46%

(Social and Cultural Services~0.0%)

1991

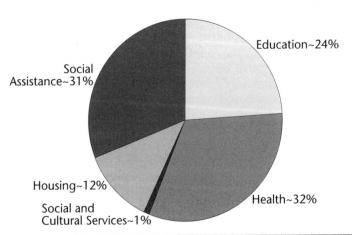

Education~24%

Social Assistance~31%

Housing~12%

Social and Cultural Services~1%

Health~32%

SOURCES: FNUAP/Costa Rica Ministry of Planning and Economic Policy (MIDE-PLAN), 1994.
Numbers rounded to nearest percentage point.

Although by the late 1970s social service expenditures consumed more than half of the state's annual budget, the overhaul of social policy was having a clear impact.[4] The proportion of Costa Rican families living in poverty had fallen from 50 percent in 1950 to 40 percent in 1971 and then down to 25 percent in 1977. The average life expectancy at birth had risen considerably, and rates of illiteracy and infant mortality were on the decline. More and more communities enjoyed access to health services and public utilities.[5] State-driven health and vaccination campaigns had eradicated many of the country's most pernicious communicable diseases and, between 1970 and 1980, deaths from infectious and parasitic diseases had fallen by 98 percent. In fact, so successful was the health care campaign in the 1970s that AID took Costa Rica off its eligibility list for health care assistance because the country had become too healthy.[6]

Combined with economic growth, the government's commitment to social development (reflected in the expansion of public social services and policies favoring wage increases) between 1950 and 1980 led to widespread social mobility that catalyzed the emergence of Costa Rica's characteristically large middle class. Unfortunately much of the improvement in socioeconomic conditions had been underwritten by foreign loans and rising budget deficits. When financial crisis hit the country in 1979, the government was forced to cut back government social services spending. Between 1981 and 1990 budget reductions, compounded by population growth, shrunk the state's per capita expenses in the health sector by 34 percent (accounting for inflation) and in education by 21 percent (Figure 3a).[7] During the 1981-90 period, the government placed more emphasis on social assistance and housing programs than on maintaining its extensive health and education programs.

Changes in the structure of social services funding reflect the reworking of social policy to prioritize those populations most adversely affected by structural adjustment. These compensatory programs—commonly called social investment funds—parallel similar developments in other Latin American countries that are undergoing World Bank-directed structural adjustment.

An early manifestation of the new compensatory emphasis in public benefits emerged in 1983 when the government proposed measures to distribute food, generate employment, build new housing, and distribute land.[8] In later years the Arias administration (1986-90), responding to demands by housing advocacy groups, launched projects to construct low-income housing and distribute vouchers for low-interest home loans. A third scheme for social compensation, initiated by the Calderón administration (1990-94), also distributed vouchers for housing, as well as for schooling and food, and created a system of day care centers, called "Community Homes," designed to enable housewives to seek employment. Additionally the Calderón government launched small and medium-sized business development projects to help generate employment.

Policymakers in the Figueres administration (1994-98) designed a program to focus state development efforts on the sixteen poorest communities in the country. Levels of poverty were mapped out geographically to determine which districts should be targeted for assistance. Figueres also outlined his Plan to Combat Poverty that aimed to eliminate obstacles that women, children, labor and other groups encounter in obtaining basic state services. A widening budget deficit and new pressures from the World Bank place the future of such new social assistance efforts in doubt.

Although the various government programs to target the poor have undoubtedly softened the impact of structural adjustment in some instances, their effect has been undermined both by partisan political efforts to win votes and by the traditional clientelism that characterizes relations between the state and the popular sectors. Such meddling characteristically sidetracks public benefits from reaching the poorest of the poor—people who could most benefit from social assistance but who have the least power to demand the state's attention.

Health

The good health of Costa Ricans—superior to that of many communities in the United States—is a product of a state-sponsored infrastructure of health services matched in Latin America only by Cuba. When compared with most other Central American countries, Costa Rica's health care advances are truly impressive. One indicator of the country's commitment to citizen health is its social security system, which covers 84 percent of Costa Ricans—easily the highest rate in the region. Latest statistics show infant deaths to be around 14 per thousand compared with 54 per thousand in neighboring Nicaragua and 18 in Panama. Life expectancy is 76 years, compared to 63 years in Nicaragua and 72 years in Panama.[9] Ninety-four percent of the population has access to potable water and 97 percent benefits from health, sewage, and sanitation services (Figure 3b).[10] In 1993 Costa Rica placed 39th among 173 countries ranked in the United Nations' living standards index.

Figure 3b
Health in Statistics

Life expectancy	76 years
Infant mortality per 1000 live births	14
Fertility (children per woman)	3.2
Daily caloric supply (as % of requirements)	121%
% of one-year-olds fully immunized	93%
Physicians per 10,000 people	12.5
Access to safe water	94%
Access to health, sewage, and sanitation services	97%
Public health expenditure as % of GDP	3%

SOURCE: Bread for the World Institute, 1994

The compensatory emphasis in social policy since the early 1980s has had palpable, detrimental effects on earlier efforts to universalize access to health and educational services. Financial reshuffling has hit emergency and preventive health care programs the hardest, as seen in the rise in contagious diseases such as measles and meningitis, an increase in cases of hepatitis and diarrhea, and outbreaks of malaria and sexually transmitted diseases. Hospital directors and social security and family assistance officials also confirm that the quality and availability of medical services have substantially deteriorated since the mid-1980s. Medicines and hospital beds are in short supply; medical attention, when available, has become routine and impersonal. At least 10 percent of hospital patients acquire new diseases during their hospital care due to budget cuts in hospital sanitary services.

The shrinking social services budget has also meant less government money for potable water systems, sewage treatment, and public health programs. As a result of fewer wells and community water facilities being installed, the percentage of Costa Ricans with potable water and sanitary facilities inside their homes is declining for the first time. The lack of public funds for trash collection and sewage treatment has translated into increased water contamination. Across-the-board cuts in social service programs contribute both to the general decline in public health and to the rise in preventable diseases. The government has acknowledged that the rise in gastrointestinal diseases, alcoholism, and drug dependency are directly attributable to the economic crisis and decaying social conditions.

Education

Costa Ricans enjoy the best public education system in Central America. Government expenditures on education as a percentage of national income are 1 percent higher than the 4 percent standard recommended by UNESCO. As one result of this commitment to education, 93 percent of Costa Ricans can read and write. In other Latin American countries, the literacy rates for men are significantly higher than those of women, while in Costa Rica the rates are the same (Figure 3c).

A qualitatively superior system of higher education also distinguishes Costa Rica. For the last few decades, there have been four public university systems: University of Costa Rica (UCR) and Na-

Figure 3c
Education in Statistics

Mean years of schooling	
Male	5.6
Female	5.8
Adult literacy (over age 15)	
Adults age 15-19	97%
Male	93%
Female	93%
% enrolled in primary schools	100%
% enrolled in secondary school	42%
% enrolled in institutions of higher learning	26%
Years to produce 6th grade student	7.5
% of national budget spent on education	25%
Public education expenditure as % of GDP	4.6%

SOURCE: US Agency for International Development (AID),1994

tional University (UNA) as well as the state-financed Technological Institute of Costa Rica (ITCR). Costa Ricans also have easy access to the State University at a Distance (UNED), a state extension/correspondence university established especially for students living in rural areas. Like many other Latin American nations, university-level institutions enjoy legal autonomy. This autonomy, which ensures freedom of expression and political activism, has been carefully observed, in contrast to other countries of the region.[11]

In recent years, a number of expensive private institutions of primary, secondary, and higher learning have blossomed around the country. The private universities concentrate on business and the sciences, and are run like corporations. The Autonomous University of Central America (UACA), founded in 1975, is the leading private university. Actually, it is a collection of different departments (law, medicine, etc.) that function as separate profitmaking enterprises. Founded by former UCR professor Guillermo Malavassi, UACA was hailed as a pro-capitalist institution in contrast to the left-leaning sentiments that characterized the national centers of higher learning during the mid-1970s. Today, UACA continues to be a center for neoliberal thought, joined by an array of other private colleges, most of which also foster conservative views about education, politics, and economics. These include Interamerican University of Puerto Rico (based in Puerto Rico), Higher School of Business Administration (ESAP), Higher Institute of Business Administration (ISAE), Technical Institute of Business Administration (ITAN), and numerous others. Recent governments have been roundly criticized for allowing higher education to slip into the hands of private ownership, gradually converting university learning into an exclusive privilege of the wealthy.

Parallel to cutbacks in health and sanitation services, the last decade and a half has seen the government's steady hacking away at the education budget. Primary and secondary schools have been the main targets of financial reduction despite a growing demand for their services. Forced to adapt, school administrators have resorted to hiring underqualified staff: nearly 25 percent of public school teachers are unlicensed. Additionally, teachers have doubled up on classrooms and reduced the length of the school day to compensate for a countrywide shortage of nearly six hundred classrooms.[12] Most schools struggle with a chronic lack of textbooks, chalkboards, paper, pencils, rulers, and other equipment. Ironically, state universities have increased their take of education funds due to a constitutional mandate that fixes a percentage of the national budget for higher learning.

Public education suffers from problems other than poor financing. The school curriculum has not been revised in over fifteen years, and deteriorating living conditions contribute to high rates of student absenteeism and slow rates of academic progress. It seems unlikely that these conditions will soon change; the only mention of education reform from the Figueres administration has involved proposals to introduce English and universalize preschool teaching in public schools.

Two Costa Ricas

Private health and educational facilities are becoming increasingly prevalent in Costa Rica. Although typically more attentive and better equipped than their public analogues, private medicine and schooling are affordable only to the wealthiest of Costa Ricans—a fact that prompts frequent commentary on the growing rift between "two Costa Ricas," rich and poor. Even government officials openly acknowledge their concern over the bipolarization of Costa Rican society along public and private lines. In a televised public service announcement, Minister of Education Eduardo Doryan has appeared hefting a tattered schoolbook in one hand and a glossy new text in the other hoping to draw attention to the growing disparity between the quality of public and private school facilities.

The displacement of public services by private enterprise suggests that a precedent is being set that will likely have grave implications for Costa Rican society by the turn of the century. In the last fifteen years the government has put little effort into expanding or even sustaining the national health, public utility, and educational infrastructure that made such impressive advances in the fight against poverty through the 1970s. The jury is still out on the degree to which this neglect is already affecting the living conditions of many Costa Ricans: AID statistics show the proportion of households living in a state of poverty increasing from 21 to 22 percent in urban areas and decreasing from to 28 to 25 percent in the countryside between 1988 and 1990.[13] A confidential study leaked from within the Ministry of Labor suggests a more austere picture however: between 1987 and 1992 the number of Costa Ricans failing to meet their basic needs rose from 21 to 28 percent of the population.[14] Most recently, Vice-President Rebeca Grynspan announced that 30-38 percent of Costa Rican families live in poverty, and 17-25 percent in extreme poverty.[15]

In the coming years, government authorities will also confront significant regional disparities in levels of poverty. The industrialized

Central Region experiences an unemployment rate of only 3.7 percent. Poor households make up 11.5 percent of its population and infant mortality stands at 12.9 per thousand. In contrast, the Central Pacific Region displays a 6.4 percent unemployment rate. More than a third of the households in Brunca are classified as poor and infant mortality in the Atlantic Huetar region is nearly 18 per thousand.

By all indications, the Costa Rican state has not yet charted a policy course that genuinely aims to close the growing gap between rich and poor. The principal challenge is how to integrate economic growth with social development in such a way that humanist concerns are not made a subsidiary and subordinate component of economic policy. Clearly neoliberal economics have been unable to achieve such a balance; and it is debatable whether any development model that assumes economic benefits from corporate investment automatically "trickle down" to poorer populations can equilibrate income patterns. What is certain, however, is that any initiative to redistribute the country's economic resources will meet with staunch opposition from the business community arguing that such programs reduce Costa Rica's competitiveness in the world system. Progressive-minded political leaders have met this objection before and countered with the argument that competitive capacity should be measured not by the affordability of the country's labor force, but rather by its quality. A skilled and well-paid population of workers, in other words, is far more productive than one that struggles daily to ensure its own survival.

Part 4

Civil Society

© Donna DeCesare/Impact Visuals

Popular Organizing

Costa Rica does not have the tradition of popular organizing seen elsewhere in Latin America. The government's attention to the basic needs of poor and working people has in many ways obviated the need for the kind of community organizing that occurs in countries where there is little government concern for the broad social welfare.

Popular organizing in other Central American countries was sparked, to a large degree, by progressive Catholic clergy, who recognized that traditional charity solutions fell far short of addressing the structural problems facing poor communities. In Costa Rica, the church hierarchy isolated itself from the progressive trends within the Latin American church and vigorously discouraged social activism on the part of its clergy. Church organizations like Catholic Action, which in other countries organized cooperatives and sponsored popular education programs, remained paternalistic charitable institutions in Costa Rica.

Despite the paucity of church-based movements, Costa Rica still displays a great diversity of organizing efforts, largely in the form of labor unions, cooperatives, community development associations, campesino organizations, and *solidarista* (solidarity) associations. Popular movements in Costa Rica are recognized legally; of 1,219 groups registered with the government, 39 percent are agricultural associations, 24 percent are communal associations, 14 percent are housing advocacy groups, 12 percent are women's associations, and a small percentage focus on issues of the environment, microenterprise development, artisanry, and fishing. Also on record are nearly 5,000 church groups, senior homes, sports clubs, and cultural clubs.[1]

The tradition of popular organizing in Costa Rica has unfolded within a political system characterized by the pursuit of democratic consensus and the assurance of certain civil liberties. Where popular mobilization has meant a collective effort to defend group interests, as in the case of labor unions and campesino organizations, demands and protests have largely been directed at the state (with the primary exception being the Banana Unions Network). Historically, the Costa Rican government has displayed a remarkable capacity to respond to conflict and forge agreements with popular-sector organizations.

The state's actions have not been limited to conflict resolution, however, but have also involved attempts to undermine popular organizations. Such was the case with the Popular Vanguard Party (PVP): rural organizations promoted by the government in the 1930s were, at least in part, a response to the PVP's history of association with banana workers and its attempt to form Peasant Leagues. The government's establishment of community development associations was a similar attempt to undermine the communist-sponsored Progressive Community Directorates.

The state has also managed to insert its influence by sponsoring institutions that coordinate community organizing activities. The state-funded Cooperative Bank and INFOCOOP (Institute for Cooperative Promotion), for example, oversee financial and promotional activities in the cooperative sector. Many in government see cooperatives and local associations as appropriate vehicles for broad-based community development. But the policies guiding government-sponsored cooperatives and community groups often aim to coopt popular movements, channeling them into activities that are less antagonistic to the government's agenda. Thus critics accuse the National Directorate of Community Development (DINADECO) of diverting grassroots initiatives into strongly hierarchical community associations that generally abstain from collaborative relationships with other popular movements.[2] Typically, those organizations that remain staunchly resistant to the state's programs and ideology are systematically excluded from political recognition.

In the 1980s, government austerity measures—the layoff of public employees, the privatization of state services, and the cutting back of public wages—sparked protests among Costa Rican labor unions, the great majority of which originate in the public sector. Nevertheless, no persistent, organized movement emerged to confront the adjustment.

Only the campesino associations mounted any sustained response to the government's new economic policies. It was in the agricultural sector where the consequences of restructuring became quickly apparent. As a result of the new economic thinking, the country began to experience food deficits, and small-scale producers were squeezed out of the farming business by pricing and credit policies. At the same time, policies promoting agroexport production had the effect of driving small producers off the land, creating a large and increasingly militant sector of landless campesinos.

As a dynamic rural movement was developing in response to government policy, the farmer associations proved adept not only at bringing many medium-size and some large farmers into the coalition but also at attracting some of the more conservative and government-linked associations of small farmers. This unity, while an indisputable strength, has been difficult to maintain and fortify due to the government's strategy of negotiating with farmer groups sector by sector. The government has also tried to isolate the most militant farmer associations, notably UPAGRA (Small Farmers Union of the Atlantic), by accusing them of being marxist-organized and financed organizations with military capabilities.[3]

The economic situation for Costa Rica's lower classes exacerbated during the 1980s, but this economic trauma did not necessarily broaden and strengthen the country's popular movement. This was due in part to the ability of the government to alleviate some of the concerns of the most vocal sectors. Another factor debilitating the popular sectors is the political sectarianism that divides community organizations, especially during election years. A low degree of popular political education also helps explain the weak state of the popular movement. Reflecting on the state of popular organizing, political analyst Manuel Rojas Bolaños observed, "The popular movement does not appear willing to endure more restrictions [austerity measures and budget cuts], but since they lack an appropriate alternative, they move like blind worms, which upon running into tiny obstacles remove some of them while others force them to redefine their route, without ever knowing where they are going."[4]

The inertia of structural adjustment and economic liberalization in Costa Rica has persuaded many popular organizations to associate themselves with the government's new development model. As actors in a developing world system, community-based initiatives are now exposed to political and economic forces more ominous and far-reaching than ever before. The fear is that by remaining resistant, even combative to structural change, popular organizations may marginalize themselves out of existence. Thus, their strategy has "changed from the protest to the proposal": rather than aggressive confrontation, community groups are attempting to propose ways in which the government can make room for their interests in implementing economic policy changes. Perhaps a subtle sign of this political neutralization is the fact that groups in the popular sector are increasingly referred to as "social" rather than "popular" organizations.

Cooperatives

Cooperatives sprouted in Costa Rica in the 1950s and expanded greatly in the 1970s. Together with the creation of communal development associations, promotion of cooperatives formed a primary thrust of the state's development program from 1948 to 1979. Between 1950 and 1970 the cooperative model played a central role in the consolidation of medium-size and small-scale farms tied to the production of coffee and sugarcane in the Central Valley and to cattle production in the northern region of the country. In 1983 there were 407 cooperatives with 200,375 registered members. By 1994 Costa Rica had 452 cooperatives embracing 326,594 members. Cooperatives constitute the largest popular organizing sector and represent nearly 32 percent of the total work force.[5]

There are three basic types of cooperative: those based on consumer goods and services, those formed to facilitate savings and credit, and productive cooperatives. Eighty percent of members join cooperatives for greater access to consumer and credit facilities. Cooperatives vary greatly in size, from the few gigantic productive organizations (Coopemontecillos, Dos Pinos, Coopesa), with advanced technologies and ample investments, to smaller and politically weaker grassroots cooperatives that generally originate in the campesino sector.

Among social organizations, large cooperatives carry the greatest weight in the national economy. According to statistics from the Institute for Cooperative Promotion (INFOCOOP), the major productive cooperatives generate 11 percent of Costa Rica's GNP.[6]

Cooperative leadership is strongly critical of the government's structural adjustment policies. Nevertheless, it concedes that, given the dearth of viable economic alternatives coming out of the popular sectors, "the healthy thing for us to do is adjust as well as possible to this movement and not align ourselves in opposition to it."[7] Clinging to the original cooperative principle of putting social ends above corporate profits—all the while relying heavily on state assistance— many cooperatives have fallen on hard times. Cooperative development steers more and more toward increased efficiency, productivity, and competitiveness in a world market. The challenge facing the cooperative sector in the future is whether it can engage this new modernist track without betraying its traditional commitment to solidarity, participation, and economic democracy.

Communal Organizations

Community organizations are integrated into a network controlled by a state institution called DINADECO (National Directorate of Community Development), which channels government resources and training to local groups known as Community Development Associations (ADCs). The ADCs generally carry out local infrastructure projects, relying on the community for necessary labor. DINADECO was created in 1968 under the Alliance for Progress, and the majority of ADCs were organized in the 1970s. Their number climbs yearly and currently includes about 1,570 separate associations.

The communal development organizational structure has become increasingly complex and includes 57 cantonal unions, 14 zonal unions, 8 federations, and the National Confederation of Communal Development Associations (CONADECO, created in 1990). Some community leaders originally opposed the idea of a national confederation out of the concern that it would become another instrument used by the state to control the popular movement.[8]

In addition to organizing community-level infrastructure projects, the ADCs promote the culture of popular organizing and the formation of community leaders around the country. Nonetheless, they have also been the target of strong criticisms, as much from within the movement as without. Detractors highlight the penetration of party politics and the state's influence in the administration of ADC programs. Their financial dependence on the government not surprisingly makes them vulnerable to political clientelism on a variety of levels. As a result, ADCs have experienced a decline in community participation and have failed to lead popular opposition to the neoliberal transformation of government.

ADC leaders have assigned priority to the implementation of projects that generate their own income and are potentially self-sustaining. Reflective of this new vision, the current director of CONADECO observed, "We now have associations that are practically businesses." An ADC in Tabarcia de Mora owns a bus company, an association in Hatillo develops training programs for women and youth, and in Paquera there is an ADC that raises goats. In other parts of the country, Community Development Associations run bakeries and manage corn and bean fields.[9] Such activities might seem to contradict the traditional purpose of ADCs, to construct community infrastructure, but a reduced dependence on the state's finances falls directly in line with the mandate of structural adjustment. Unfortunately, economic independence has not entirely rid the ADCs of external political influence. Such a transformation would require a fundamental reworking of DINADECO, which the state is unlikely to support.

Campesino Organizations

Campesino organizations consist mostly of small-scale coffee producers, subsistence farming peasants, and agricultural laborers.[10] In addition to rural cooperatives, campesino groups take the form of agrarian unions, the Cantonal Agrarian Centers, and independent associations of farmers.

Farm labor unions draw on a membership of more than 43,000 people, mostly land-poor farmers who periodically work for wages, and, to a lesser degree, salaried agricultural laborers. The dominant union for salaried agricultural workers is the Banana Unions Network, which formed in response to worker health problems that resulted from pesticide use in transnational banana companies.

The Cantonal Agrarian Centers (CAC), formed in the 1960s, unite around 15,000 farmers. The sixty-five CACs are divided into 8 regional federations and overseen by the National Confederation of Cantonal Agricultural Centers (CNCAC).[11] Farmers and government officials work together in the centers to, among other things, facilitate the purchase and sale of fertilizers, and promote the commercialization of grains, the purchase of beans, and the supply of seeds. The CNCAC also provides technical and financial support to the CACs for support services and training of CAC members.

As with most other social movements, campesino organizations are constantly searching for greater autonomy from the state and major political parties. Until the mid-1980s, struggle in the campesino sector was led by the agrarian unions and their federations. Since then, independent organizations have seized the initiative, committing themselves to agendas that they describe as "more campesino" in nature.[12] The best-known examples of independent organizations include the National Union of Small and Medium Farmers (UPANACIONAL, 18,000 members) created in 1981 as the largest agricultural union in the country; the Small Farmers Union of the Atlantic (UPAGRA), founded in 1978 and the driving force behind campesino protests in 1986 and 1987; the Independent Agricultural Producers Union of Pérez Zeledón (UPIAV); and the Campesino Council of Justice and Development (CCJD), created in 1990 and recently active in campesino land seizures. Additionally, agricultural producers across the country have coalesced to form nearly 470 smaller independent associations that are mostly focused on issues of local concern.

Although buffeted by the tides of changing government, campesinos have waged a constant struggle for cultivable land since the 1950s. The last national census, conducted in 1984, revealed that 13 percent of property owners possessed 75 percent of Costa Rica's arable land. Following five years of intense mobilization and protest, campesinos convinced the Institute for Agrarian Development (IDA) in 1986 to distribute 106,625 hectares to almost 9,000 land-hungry rural families.[13]

The repercussions of the first structural adjustment program, signed in 1985, were felt almost immediately in the campesino sector. Farmers noted the state's waning interest in basic grains production as well as dwindling access to credit and technological support for small-scale production. Lack of technology, capital, and know-how have made it difficult for most small-scale farmers to adjust to the neo-export emphasis in agriculture policy. Financial crises have driven many rural dwellers from their lands and into the large and growing rural labor reserve that sustains commercial, export-oriented plantations.

Facilitated by a tradition of interorganizational cooperation that dates back to the 1950s, labor groups, independent associations, co-operatives, and agricultural centers have developed a common strategy to confront the process of structural adjustment. Among the principles to guide future organizing efforts, campesino leaders highlight the need to promote self-sufficiency and sustainable development in farming communities, to regulate export industry so that it remains in the hands of domestic producers, and to support both vertical and regional integration in the areas of production, processing, and marketing.[14] Above all, the campesino organizations stress their intent to participate in future negotiations between the state and international financing organizations.

A final and growing factor in rural Costa Rica is the renewed movement of landless rural dwellers to claim land. In their takeovers of uncultivated private land and challenges to the government's Institute for Agrarian Development (IDA), landless campesino families have been met with escalating repression, both from private and official security forces. In September 1994, dozens of campesinos were wounded in a confrontation with police after 127 poor, rural families occupied the Rincón Grande de Pavas farm on the outskirts of San José. The group was protesting the government's plans to move them from the farm after having been relocated once already from a nearly finished housing project in the capital city.[15]

Labor Unions

The labor movement in Costa Rica can be traced to the last century when workers formed mutual-aid societies and the government began regulating workers and professionals. In the 1890s the Catholic Church took an interest in labor organizing as a way to form a popular base for the Catholic Union Party. Later the church supported labor unions mainly as an antidote to the mounting strength of communist labor unions. The country's first strikes and open labor conflict involved Chinese and Italian workers contracted in the 1880s to build the country's railroads.

It was not until 1913, with the formation of the General Confederation of Workers (CGT), that the country gained its first true labor organization. The Communist Party, formed in 1931, pushed labor organizing to new levels of militancy and success, beginning with the 1934 strike that brought United Fruit to a standstill. The communist-backed Costa Rican Workers Confederation (CTCR) grew steadily, giving the communist party major influence in national politics. Pressure from the leftist unions resulted, for example, in the institution during the 1940s of the Costa Rican Labor Code, including protective guarantees and a system of bonuses and severance pay.

Beginning in the mid-1940s two interrelated forces—social democratic tendencies associated with the AFL-CIO and Social Christian elements associated with the Catholic Church—struggled to undermine the influence of the Communist Party among the nation's working class. The church, for example, organized the Rerum Novarum Workers Confederation of Costa Rica (CCTRN) in 1945 to withdraw worker support from the leftist-backed CTCR. The international department of the AFL-CIO, in close cooperation with the CIA and U.S. State Department, soon established links with the anticommunist CCTRN. After the victory of social democrat José Figueres in 1948, the CTCR was dismantled and the Communist Party outlawed. At the same time, Figueres and the new government promoted the CCTRN (later reorganized as the CCTD). An international network comprising the AFL-CIO-associated Interamerican Regional Organization of Workers (ORIT) and the AID-financed American Institute for Free Labor Development (AIFLD) also threw its considerable support behind the CCTD.

Leftist unions were not permitted to operate again until 1953, at which time the Costa Rican General Workers Confederation (CGTC) was established. Once again, it was the unions associated with the reconstituted Popular Vanguard Party (PVP) that began to dominate the field of trade union and peasant organizing as the CCTRN gradually weakened. The Catholic Church lost interest in the formation of Christian unions after the death in 1952 of Archbishop Sanabria. For its part, the PLN, while favoring the CCTRN and later the CCTD, did little to promote trade unionism but instead opted to promote the cooperative movement.

Benefiting from the conciliatory policies of the reformist state, national economic growth and, above all, the rapid expansion of the state apparatus, the union movement grew steadily in the 1960s and

1970s. The strengthening of organized labor was impressive, rising from just 2.6 percent of the work force in 1963 to 15.7 percent two decades later. Internal divisions, the inability to formulate a common political/economic vision, the rise of the *solidarismo* movement, and the near disappearance of banana labor unions contributed to the stagnation of the Costa Rican labor movement of the 1980s.

The strength of the labor movement even at its height was undermined by its concentration in the public sector and virtual absence in private industry. A total lack of legal protections in the private sector exposes labor leaders to the threat of immediate layoff if they are suspected of attempting to rally workers. In 1992 only 7 percent of the private sector work force was organized in unions. Costa Rican unions are strong only in the large public sector, where 60 percent of government employees are union members.

The labor movement is characterized by the proliferation of small unions and the lack of labor unity. The country has 424 unions and six union confederations. These confederations represent less than three-quarters of union members since 30 percent belong to independent unions, and 43 percent of all labor unions are independent.[16] The Permanent Worker Council (CPT), formed in 1986 to embrace all of the labor confederations and independent unions, is the latest and most successful attempt at labor unity. The fracturing of the Communist Party at the beginning of the 1980s and the disappearance of leftist currents in labor organizing in the 1990s reduced its influence.

In September 1992 three confederations united to reconstitute the CCTRN: the Costa Rican Confederation of Democratic Workers (CCTD), the National Confederation of Workers (CNT), and the Authentic Confederation of Democratic Workers (CATD). The CCTD was an affiliate of the International Confederation of Free Trade Unions (ICFTU) and politically close to the PLN. In the mid-1960s CCTD shed its ties to the Christian labor movement in favor of its association with the ICFTU and AIFLD. The CATD formed in 1971 in a split with CCTD over alleged interference by ORIT/AIFLD advisers.

The CNT was formed in 1983 by AIFLD organizers wary of the increasing independence of the CCTD. Through its Campesino Strengthening Project, AIFLD works with CNT to support a peasant organization called FEDETAICO, which promotes nontraditional agroexport production by conservative campesino groups.

The group of organizations composing the CCTRN follows a social democratic orientation and forms the majority component of Costa Rican unionism, including 35 percent of unions and 46 percent of union members.[17] It is followed in order of numerical importance by the non-confederated or independent unions, which represent 43 percent of all unions and 30 percent of union participants. Among the strongest independent organizations are the Public Sector Workers Union (ANEP), with some 10,000 members, and the National Teachers Association (ANDE), which is the country's most powerful labor organization with 26,000 members. In 1987 ANDE joined with two smaller teachers' unions to form the Inter-Magisterial Council.

The Confederation of Costa Rican Workers (CTC) represents 6 percent of unions and 11 percent of union members. It was formed in 1972 as an evolution of Social Christian unionism, which formally took hold in 1964 at the initiative of the Latin American Confederation of Workers (CLAT), an international affiliate of the World Confederation of Labor (WCL). In 1993 a group of independent unions along with the CTC formed a new confederation called the CLAT Confederation.[18]

In the 1990s the labor movement faces an array of obstacles, including the following:

- Effective loss of worker rights to collective bargaining.
- Restrictive government policies.
- Constraints imposed by the Costa Rican Labor Code, whose benefits are applicable only to those labor conflicts judged legal by the Supreme Court.
- Rise of the *solidarismo* movement.
- Lack of effective labor movement unity.
- Continued ability of government to coopt sectors of the labor movement.

Collective bargaining is waning as a method for resolving labor conflicts. The most severe blow to collective bargaining rights came in 1979 when the government passed the Public Administration Law, which restricts the right of public employees to negotiate contracts. Although the government has respected unions that predated the 1979 law, it has steadfastly refused to recognize the rights of new public employee unions to negotiate contracts. Direct agreements between workers and companies in lieu of collective bargaining arrangements are common in the private sector. The government has further restricted the strategy options of public sector unions with the 1984 Financial Stability Law, which additionally narrows the few instances when government institutions can negotiate directly with their employees.

Another threat to public sector employees comes from the government's agreements with international financial organizations to reduce public spending and privatize state institutions. This trend is especially threatening since some 15 percent of the country's labor force and 65 percent of organized labor falls within the public sector.[19] Leading the opposition to privatization are workers of the Costa Rican Electricity Institute (ICE).

The union movement slowed down in the 1980s while experiencing several major setbacks, notably the switch of many banana workers to the *solidarismo* movement. Unionists looking for hopeful signs can find them in the achievement of a certain degree of unity through the CPT and the success of some unions in winning limited demands. As a whole, though, the union movement is characterized by a lack of both militancy and a strong political analysis of the national crisis.

In contrast with the breadth of labor activity found in the public sector, private enterprise is characterized by the relative lack of union organizing, due in part to the repression of union organizers. Persecution of labor leaders and other violations of the freedom to organize have been documented by the AFL-CIO and the International Confederation of Free Labor Organizations (CIOSL). Despite the apparent gains that labor has made in pushing for changes in labor legislation, over the years governments have failed to honor many of the agreements they signed on to.

In 1988 the CIOSL presented to the International Organization of Work (OIT) a document in support of union complaints regarding constraints to labor organizing, the legal vulnerability of labor leaders, and the government's favoritism towards *solidarista* associations. In response to the accusations, the Costa Rican government agreed not to honor collective bargaining agreements made with the *solidarista* associations and to offer unions effective protections against all antilabor activities.[20]

In May 1991, representatives of the AFL-CIO, in conjunction with the CTRN and the Interamerican Regional Organization of Workers (ORIT), met with Costa Rican officials to express their concern that labor standards outlined in the Generalized System of Preferences (GSP) were being violated. The meeting was partly prompted by admissions on the part of Costa Rica's vice-minister of labor that, "It is absolutely impossible to create a labor union in the private sector in Costa Rica." The government's willingness to implement changes in labor law, however, persuaded the AFL-CIO not to press for a repeal of Costa Rica's preferential trade status with the United States. Formal agreements were signed a year later and included the government's commitment to expand legal protections for labor organizing, modify the punishments imposed on strikers by the Costa Rican Penal Code, establish collective bargaining agreements, and submit a law in the Legislative Assembly that would prohibit *solidarista* associations from engaging in collective bargaining.[21]

Nevertheless, government functionaries admitted to the AFL-CIO in 1993 that, despite their good intentions, the government had accomplished little real change in ensuring that labor rights were honored. It was then that the AFL-CIO formally petitioned for Washington to revoke Costa Rica's trade privileges through the GSP and the Caribbean Basin Initiative as well as guarantees of the U.S. Overseas Private Investment Corporation (OPIC).[22] Threatened with the imposition of tariffs amounting to $81 million, the Costa Rican government felt genuinely pressured for the first time. In the midst of mutual recriminations and pressure from business sectors, the government negotiated a series of reforms with the AFL-CIO at the end of the 1993. It remains to be seen whether greater legal protections and freedom to organize will in fact affect the development of unionism in the private sector.

The public sector has also been the focus of legal reforms affecting labor. The recently proposed Public Sector Democratization Law seeks to privatize those institutions considered nonessential to the task of governing by putting them into the hands of cooperatives and other forms of labor association. The proposed Unemployment Compensation Transformation Law aims to create a capital fund consisting of revenues that decentralized organizations—the *solidarista* associations, the unions, the cooperatives, or the national banking system—would manage. This controversial proposal was met by immediate opposition from the business community and proponents of *solidarismo* because it would break their monopoly access to severance pay. If approved, these reforms will open up new possibilities for the development of unionism and its incursion into different fields, like business ventures and the provision of services to union members.

Solidarismo Takes Off

Solidarismo is a philosophy of worker-owner cooperation formulated by Alberto Marten in Costa Rica in 1947. It is designed as an alternative to class confrontation, unionism, and collective bargaining:

Solidarismo conceives of the company as an ethical economic association and private property as a keystone of society that fulfills the social objective of redistribution. Thus, the application of *solidarista* principles to business results from an understanding of the company as an expression of the harmonious relation between capital and labor, which need each other mutually to achieve the common objectives to produce more and distribute more.[23]

In practice, *solidarismo* takes the form of associations in which businesses and workers alike contribute to the formation of credit and investment projects. The funds come from worker savings and investment by the company owner of the employee's future severance pay.

By 1959 around 70 *solidarista* associations had sprung up around the country, but in the two succeeding decades, as the social state grew, the *solidarista* movement stalled. It was in the 1980s, in the context of economic crisis and an emergent model of development centered on structural adjustment, that the *solidarista* experiment had its greatest success, growing faster than any other form of social organization.

Solidarismo is largely a creature of the private sector: 96 percent of *solidarista* associations and 92 percent of their members originate in private enterprise, primarily industry and commerce. Lately *solidarismo* has also established associations in the public sector that account for almost 6 percent of *soladarista* membership.

The *solidarista* movement has received strong support from the state and diverse political and social groups. In 1984 the Legislative Assembly approved a law granting the *solidarista* associations, in detriment to the labor movement, jurisdiction over operations of credit, savings, investment and any other activity that generates profits and that foments ties with and between labor and capital.[24]

During the 1980s, while the union movement stagnated, the number of *solidarista* affiliates quintupled. By the end of the decade, *solidarismo* could rightly boast that its membership rivaled that of competing union movements.

As a result of rapid growth in the 1980s, the *solidarista* movement in 1992 expanded to 1,250 associations with over 134,000 members, representing nearly 13 percent of the labor force.[25] The base of the movement has been the manufacturing sector in the San José metropolitan area, where labor organization in the private sector is practically nonexistent. Since 1985 *solidarismo* has also made impressive inroads in the agricultural sector, especially the banana industry. *Solidarista* associations have all but replaced the leftist banana workers' unions that until the 1980s were responsible for organizing prolonged, sometimes violent strikes in demand of better salaries and working conditions. The movement is also growing in the commercial sector where, for the same reasons as in industry, there are no labor organizations. Over 90 percent of the country's U.S-based transnationals, including Firestone, McDonald's, Coca-Cola, RJ Reynolds, IBM, and Standard Brands, sponsor *solidarista* associations.[26]

The benefits of *solidarismo* have not all been illusory. Aside from the reluctance to involve themselves in labor-management strife, workers often choose to stay with *solidarista* associations for some tangible rewards. They point to the cheap loans, savings plans, social events, and medical, recreational, and educational facilities. Such advantages are especially attractive to workers because of the economic adversity they normally face.

Within the *solidarista* associations, labor relations are generally sustained through direct arrangements between a worker and employer. In the case of dire conflict, representatives of the workers and of the company meet unofficially. Some *solidarista* associations have created "Permanent Worker's Committees" that have assumed an active role in establishing collective agreements that compete directly with the activities of labor organizations.

In addition to taking over the functions of a labor organization and of offering a multiplicity of services to their members, some *solidarista* associations have also become private companies, engaging in profitable investments like the purchase of bonds in the financial market, buying stocks in the business in which members work, or even forming peripheral companies that supply major businesses with some good or service. In 1993 the capital held by the *solidarista* associations stood at nearly $266 million.

Although economic democracy through participation in corporate capital is a main objective of *solidarismo*, its accomplishments in this regard are limited. In 1993, only 7 percent of the associations had engaged in corporate investments.[27]

Solidarismo comprises two tendencies. One emanates from the John XXIII Social School directed by Father Claudio Solano, a conservative Catholic priest. This faction of *solidarismo* likens the movement to the social philosophy of the Catholic Church and has focused on the manufacturing and banana transnationals in Costa Rica. It sees *solidarismo* as a "holy crusade" against communist-inspired unionism and class struggle. With a staff of over four dozen organizers, the school not only helps organize new associations but also is a center for training for the entire movement.

The other *solidarista* current, founded in 1980 and backed by Costa Rican entrepreneurs, is known as the Costa Rican Solidarista Union (SURSUM). Unlike the John XXIII School, SURSUM does not promote the purported religious foundations and objectives of *solidarismo*. SURSUM's position is that unions advocate class struggle while *solidarista* associations promote "not a class struggle but a solidarity among men."

The Costa Rican labor confederations joined together in 1987 to create the National Union Commission on Solidarismo (COSNAS). Unions have also done extensive research and analysis of their adversary through the Service Commission for Labor Growth (ASEPROLA), labor's main source of information about *solidarismo*. Opposition to *solidarismo* has arisen not only in response to *solidarismo*'s own growth but also in reaction to the movement's increasingly aggressive attempts to undermine unions by collaborating with unionized companies and by functioning as unions themselves in arranging direct wage agreements with employers. Unions complain that companies fire unionized workers, for example, to make way for *solidarista* associations.

Solidarismo also faces internal opposition as members of *solidarista* associations complain that the associations are undemocratic and lack adequate financial controls by worker representatives. Some observers predict increasing radicalization among the associations as companies fail to live up to promises to protect worker interests and as workers fall further and further behind in wage levels and in the quality of working conditions. There is also concern building among the *solidarista* associations that some companies may never be able to give retiring workers their severance pay due to poor investments and bankruptcies. One critic quipped, "*Solidarismo* is like Alka-Seltzer. Once the initial fizz is gone, the workers will be left with an empty glass and a flat taste in their mouths."[28] Ironically, office employees of the Costa Rican Solidarista Union have formed their own union to defend labor rights that they allege are being violated.

From its base in Costa Rica, *solidarismo* is spreading north to Guatemala, Honduras, and El Salvador. In 1985 the Supreme Solidarista Council of the Americas, based in Guatemala, was founded to promote *solidarismo* throughout the region. Organizers from the John XXIII Social School have traveled throughout the region as part of organizing campaigns sponsored by area business owners. The regionalization of *solidarismo* has received essential backing from such rightwing political leaders as William Middendorf (director of the Middendorf Commission for Peace and Economic Justice in Central America and a member of the Committee of Santa Fe, a conservative U.S. policy institute) and Curtin Winsor, Jr. (ambassador to Costa Rica, 1983-85).

Winsor, dubbed the "ambassador of *solidarismo*," heralded the movement as "perhaps the most original and significant ideological Latin American contribution to the West."[29] Both Winsor and Middendorf have been at the forefront of a drive to promote *solidarismo* as both an economic and ideological paradigm for Central America, and for such other geopolitical hot spots as the Philippines and South Africa. In particular, they encourage the integration of stock-ownership and profitsharing plans into the *solidarismo* movement to hasten its trajectory.

In 1988 strong opposition to *solidarismo* arose from the World Congress of the International Confederation of Free Trade Unions (ICFTU), a social-democratic confederation with which the AFL-CIO is associated. The ICFTU charged that *solidarismo*, as practiced in

Costa Rica, violated the standards set by the International Labor Organization (ILO), especially in regard to workers' rights to union membership and collective bargaining. While the U.S. government has favorably regarded and even financially supported *solidarismo*, it has also traditionally supported the operations of ICFTU, causing a mild dilemma for foreign policymakers.

With the installment of the Clinton administration, Costa Rican labor initiatives enjoy greater political receptivity in the United States than they have for over a decade. As the AFL-CIO successfully illustrated, threats like the removal of Costa Rica's preferential trade status can now be brought to bear with greater confidence that officials in the United States will respond as international accords direct them. Labor leaders are hoping this signals a new era in efforts at union organizing.

The Business Lobby

Costa Rica's business community organizes itself into industry-specific associations (including coffee production, bananas, sugar, and a host of different industrial products) and sector-specific chambers (agriculture, commerce, industry, etc.). These associations and chambers function as pressure groups to ensure that government responds to the various interests of the business community. Business leadership culminates in the Costa Rican Union of Business Chambers and Associations (UCCAEP) which, in 1992, consisted of 26 different chambers, 9 associations, one federation of chambers, and a foundation. On some issues, the business community stands relatively united, but different political and financial interests mean that various sectors take different positions on such issues as trade liberalization and deregulation.

The National Chamber of Agriculture and Animal Husbandry (CNAA) serves as the main voice of the agricultural sector, uniting medium- and large-landholding farmers, agroindustrialists, and merchants. The CNAA has maintained that the import-substitution development strategy of the 1960s and 1970s benefited the industrial sector at the expense of agricultural development. It is for this reason that the CNAA has backed recent structural adjustment policies that dismantle the historical protection of the industrial sector and liberate the agricultural sector from tariffs and policies that have impeded its development. Although the agricultural chamber has also backed the neoliberal reforms of government (privatization, deregulation, etc.), it has at the same time insisted that the government undertake programs to soften the socioeconomic impact provoked by recent structural transformations in rural areas. It also believes that the government should be cautious about proceeding too rapidly with free trade policies that may result in reduced national production.[30] It has, for example, shown only marginal interest in participating in commissions organized by the Ministry of Foreign Commerce to negotiate a free trade treaty with Mexico and promote Costa Rica's membership in GATT.[31]

For the most part, CNAA is dedicated to defending the interests of traditional agroexporters and of domestic food producers. Capitalist producers in the basic grains (especially rice) and cattle industries, both of which previously benefited from consumer subsidies and expansive government credit offerings, have voiced ardent opposition to economic liberalization. The government, however, has largely ignored the protests and demands of these producers.

Exporters of coffee and bananas feel similarly neglected because of the policy emphasis on the promotion of nontraditional exports. They argue that taxes on traditional exports effectively subsidize the incentives given to nontraditional agroexporters. Despite their declining economic clout, banana and coffee interests continue to form an influential political bloc with key connections in government. During the Calderón administration (1990-94), they strongly influenced the PUSC's selection for second vice-president. A coffee producer himself, Arnoldo López-Echandi dedicated his four years in office to advocating domestically and internationally for the Costa Rican coffee industry. In the Figueres administration, coffee producers have engaged the government in a fight to repeal the tax on coffee exports, claiming that it is discriminatory and even unconstitutional.

Between 1990 and 1994 Roberto Rojas, member of a wealthy Costa Rican family with historical ties to the banana industry, served as the minister of foreign commerce. Motivated by recent losses due to the EU's imposition of banana quotas, banana producers persuaded the government to convert their debts with the national bank from dollars to *colones*.

Perhaps the most vocal business group in the public debate surrounding national development is the Costa Rican Chamber of Industries (CIC). Conceived in the economic ferment of import-substitution industrialization and of the developing Central American Common Market, the CIC represents the country's industrial sector that produces for local and regional markets. Although the industrial chamber does not entirely oppose economic liberalization, it maintains that there is a decided governmental bias against economic sectors that do not export. Furthermore, it believes that government policies prevent domestic manufacturing industries from participating in the new development model on a par with the agricultural sector and foreign industry. One of the chamber's principal campaigns has been to oppose the accelerated elimination of tariffs on foreign capital and to demand a structural adjustment in industry that is both uniform and comprehensive. They insist that, in spite of government reform, the state should provide a program of incentives to enable industrialists to adjust their factories and production processes to the demands of the new development model. Unconditional, rapid liberalization of the economy, they argue, will lead to the ruin of national industry.

Dissatisfied with CIC's lack of initiative in promoting new exports and its continued focus on industries that produce for the domestic market, a group of business owners, mostly exporters of nontraditional products (fruits, ornamental plants, textiles, etc.), formed a splinter group in 1980 called the Costa Rican Chamber of Exporters (CADEXCO).[32] The group has played an active role in recent business lobbying efforts. CADEXCO officials accepted an invitation by the Ministry of Foreign Commerce to participate in free trade negotiations with Mexico, Colombia, Venezuela, and the United States. CADEXCO also withdrew from the Costa Rican Union of Business Chambers and Associations (UCCAEP) after it failed to support an initiative to improve and expand dock facilities in the port town of Limón.

The Limón incident also serves to illustrate UCCAEP's deteriorating ability to provide a single, unitary voice representing the interests of the Costa Rican business community. The diverse agendas characterizing the business associations and chambers in the wake of economic liberalization have become too complex and contradictory for one overarching organization to embrace.

Media

Costa Rica enjoys a free press, but it is dominated by the ideological right. While there is no censorship or suppression of the press in the country, it is difficult to find news that is not filtered through the stridently rightwing convictions of the owners of the major media.[33] The nation's largest daily newspaper, *La Nación*, sets the tone and direction of most news coverage in Costa Rica with its circulation of 75,000 every morning.

La Nación is more than a newspaper. It is a media complex. It publishes a half dozen magazines, including the prominent *Perfil* and *Rumbo*, and is linked to the cable station Cablecolor. Stockholders of *La Nación* also hold interests in the daily newspaper *La República*, Radio Monumental, and Radio Mil.

La Nación was also close to the Nicaraguan contras and served as a voice for their cause throughout Latin America. It distributed a weekly supplement called *Nicaragua Hoy*, directed from Miami by Pedro Joaquín Chamorro (son of Pedro Joaquín Chamorro, the former editor of *La Prensa* who was assassinated for his anti-Somoza views, and of Violeta Chamorro, the new U.S.-backed president of Nicaragua). *La Nación* is the country's preeminent source of news and opinion. The other media, especially the radio and television news, follow the lead of *La Nación* in reactions to news events and public policies. This is a phenomenon that close observers call the "news of consensus" in Costa Rica.

Sharing this conservative consensus are the two other dailies, *La Prensa Libre* and *La República*. Both newspapers emerged as alternatives to *La Nación*, but have moved to the right since their founding and now share its uncompromising conservatism. The morning paper, *La República*, for example, was founded in the 1950s to provide an alternative to the anti-Figueres focus of *La Nación*. It now has a circulation of 55,000 and is slightly less conservative than *La Nación*. *La Prensa Libre*, an afternoon paper with a circulation of

45,000, appeared in the 1960s as a second alternative. The ideological cohesion of the press represents the degree to which the most reactionary elements of the capitalist class have come to dominate the country's information business. The lengths to which the media will go to soil the credibility of those who differ with its worldview was exemplified in the late 1980s by repeated reports in *La Prensa Libre* claiming that the country's campesino organizations were really "paramilitary, subversive" organizations.

The progressive community in Costa Rica commonly refers to what it sees as the ideological domination and control of the country by the rightwing media. "In Costa Rica, we don't have repression with bullets, we have control by the news," observed *Semanario Universidad*'s Carlos Morales.

Three smaller papers—*Semanario Universidad, Esta Semana,* and *The Tico Times*—offer a more liberal view, but their influence is limited by their relatively small circulation. *Semanario Universidad,* the official paper of the University of Costa Rica, has gained an international reputation for its coverage of politics and the arts. It is characterized by its anti-imperialist and distinctly leftist editorial stance. *The Tico Times,* owned and edited by Richard and Dery Dyer, was established as an English language weekly to serve the retired and tourist communities. In late 1988 the newsweekly *Esta Semana* appeared on the stands, and was welcomed by many Costa Ricans tired of the sharply skewed reporting and analysis of the three dailies.

Radio stations abound, yet offer little diversity, relying on regurgitated news from the three dailies. Radio Reloj boasts the most listeners, and it bolsters the conservative consensus sweeping Costa Rica with its daily news programs and its influential noon editorial called *La Opinión.* The news station Radio Monumental is at least as conservative and faithfully reflects the rightist opinions of its owners. An exception to the conformity of the radio news is the Sunday morning program *La Patada* on Radio Sonora, which offers criticism in a humorous vein and a wide array of viewpoints. Many radio stations carry Voice of America (VOA) and other U.S. Information Service (USIS) programs in Costa Rica, including Radio Costa Rica, which devotes about half its broadcast time to VOA programming. VOA's *Buenos Días, América,* is fed to 28 radio stations in Costa Rica, while some 17 stations broadcast other VOA package programs.

Ideological variety in the world of radio was severely undermined by the 1980 bombing of a new radio station that provided listeners with international news from a leftist perspective. The most liberal station currently broadcasting is Radio América Latina, which has proved responsive to the concerns of the popular movement.

Over 90 percent of Costa Rican households have one or more television sets, on which they can receive a half dozen local stations and foreign cable programming. Cablecolor, the local cable service, broadcasts the U.S. government's daily *Arnet* program as well as CNN's 24-hour news service. Channel 7 leads the others in terms of viewers, and is trying to assert full control of the medium through the professionalization of its *Telenoticias* news program. Channel 7, formerly owned by ABC, is of the same ideological stripe as the major print media.

Perhaps because of its uniquely left-of-center perspective, the Channel 4 news program NC4 has gained great popularity in recent years. In the past electoral campaign (1993-94), NC4 scored a major success with Costa Rican TV watchers when it cast a well-known leftist intellectual to host a year-long program of electoral interviews and political analysis. Bringing up the rear of progressive programming, Channel 13, a public station founded by the PLN during a previous stint in power, also offers a more liberal take on current events, complemented by a wide array of cultural programming.

In contrast with the malaise of political passivity that seems to have overtaken popular organizations in recent years, the media is becoming more aggressive in its interrogation of government officials suspected of incompetence, corruption, and influence peddling. Much like television programming in the United States, investigative journalism has swept through the various popular media like a rock music fad. Debates and interviews homing in on the intimate details of the lives and business dealings of major party political candidates dominated the press' coverage of the last election. Following several controversial reports surrounding *liberacionista* candidate José María Figueres, the PLN demanded the resignation of journalists from *La República* and *Telenoticias*—to which the media organizations responded with accusations of a PLN cover up. Although the news programs have cast themselves as instruments of the public's right to the truth, many have pointed out the intrusive and opportunistic attitude behind journalism that saves no one and nothing from scrutiny and runs roughshod over an individual's right to privacy.

Religion

Roman Catholicism is the dominant religion in Costa Rica. The Catholic Church is also the society's most powerful institution after the government itself. While its base has been seriously undermined in the last 20 years by the evangelical movement, Catholicism still functions as the *de facto* state religion. The Catholic Church played a central role in shaping the social democratic ideology in Costa Rica. It has been instrumental in legitimizing the social welfare state, maintaining a lid on popular organizing, and propagating an ideology of anticommunism.

The development of the modern church can be traced back to 1940 when Monsignor Sanabria became archbishop of San José and brought with him a new vision of the church's role in society. Under Sanabria's reign, the church promoted several charitable and activist lay organizations including Catholic Action, Young Catholic Workers (JOC), and the Rerum Novarum Workers Confederation of Costa Rica. This new social activism of the church coincided with the Social Christian reforms promoted by the Calderón government in the 1940s, and the archbishop was drawn into an unlikely alliance with the government and the communist Popular Vanguard Party in backing these social reforms.[34]

With the ascent of the PLN in the 1950s, the Catholic Church once again withdrew from the political arena, while still supporting the Figueres government. This new political conservatism and the country's isolation from progressive trends within the Latin American church became evident in 1968, when the Archbishop of San José abstained from signing the Medellín document, which affirmed "the option for the poor." The social concern and intellectual vigor of the Sanabria tenor were lost to history. Instead, anticommunism became the prevailing theme of church homilies—despite the lack of a real threat within the country. The hierarchy, as part of this hardened anticommunism and suspicion of social activism, discouraged and at times denounced those members of the clergy who associated with the popular movement. At the end of the 1970s the conservatism of the Costa Rican church stood in marked contrast to the revitalization of the church in many other parts of Central America. According to Andrés Opazo Bernales, the author of *Costa Rica: La Iglesia Católica y el Orden Social*, the following tendencies distinguished the church at the turn of the decade:

- Lack of attention to social problems (for example: unemployment and high cost of living) generated by modern capitalist development.
- Close cooperation with the state in social work, characterized by the church's paternalistic nature.
- Support of a spiritualist approach to religious belief, in contrast to the more socially rooted theology promoted by the Medellín Conference.
- Suppression of dissidents within the church.[35]

The advent of domestic economic crisis and political upheaval in the region pushed the Catholic Church in Costa Rica out of its lethargy into assuming a more active social and political role. With the appointment of Monsignor Román Arrieta as archbishop, the church once again became an active ally of the PLN-controlled government under Monge and Arias. The church recognized that social problems had to be addressed if society was to remain stable, yet it chose to address the deepening economic crisis with charity rather than suggesting structural changes. As Opazo Bernales observed, Arrieta, a long-time PLN activist, talked more about social problems but always within the context of the PLN and the reformist government. In Costa Rica, the "option for the poor" mandate was translated into increased charity and government reforms.

Harmony between rich and poor and between church and state has been the ideology promoted by the church hierarchy. Its endorsement of the *solidarismo* movement, its promotion of such welfare organizations as CARITAS, and the integration of Catholic clergy into government institutions like INFOCOOP (the government's cooperative institute) exemplified this cautious theology. Arrieta entwined the church in the national politic, appearing routinely alongside of the president and placing the power and credibility of the church behind the government. He also provided strong backing for the government's and the media's condemnation of the Sandinistas.

While the church's ties with government strengthened in the 1980s, its hold on Costa Rican society has waned. Although nearly 85 percent of the population is Catholic, as elsewhere in Central America, Costa Ricans are eclectic believers, whose most fervent expressions of faith are evoked during Holy Week and at the baptism, marriage, or death of family members.[36] Over 80 percent of Costa Rican Catholics do not attend mass regularly.[37] Cultural Catholicism has not been able to resist the rise of the evangelical movement, spearheaded by pentecostals. To some degree, however, the incursion of evangelical churches into traditional Catholic territory has spawned a charismatic movement that incorporates the emotionalism and personal renewal aspects of pentecostal faith into Catholicism. Within the Catholic Church, there do exist communities and clergy that espouse a theology of liberation, but the institutional church isolates and represses this tendency while promoting a more spiritualistic religion.

Rise of the Evangelical Movement

Evangelical churches, which accounted for 1 percent of Costa Ricans in 1949, made rapid advances since 1965 to encompass about 16 percent of the population by the mid-1980s.[38] These churches spread throughout Costa Rica from their 19th century base among the West Indian population of the Atlantic Coast.[39] Today, the predominant evangelical churches are the Assemblies of God, Seventh Day Adventists, Pentecostal Holiness Church, Church of the Nazarene, Association of Bible Churches of Costa Rica, Association of Christian Churches, and the Fundamentalist Baptists. There are over 115 different evangelical organizations in the country, most of which experienced significant growth in the 1980s. In San José, the number of evangelical congregants doubled between 1983 and 1986.[40]

Three mainline Protestant denominations—Methodists, Baptists, and Anglicans—have the longest history in Costa Rica (dating from the mid-1880s) but currently comprise only a small group of followers. Beginning in the 1890s, U.S. missionary Bible societies began setting up missions among the Spanish-speaking society. In addition to the Central American Mission and the Latin American Mission, the Seventh Day Adventists also established missions at this time, and are today one of the largest evangelical churches in the country.

The Latin American Mission, which entered the country in 1921, was the driving force in exposing Costa Rica to the evangelical movement. Its sponsorship of Billy Graham's Caribbean Crusade in 1958 and the Evangelism-in-Depth campaign in 1961 had the effect of establishing evangelical faith as a credible alternative to Catholicism. The Mission also contributed substantially to the creation of an evangelical infrastructure in Costa Rica, having founded numerous institutions including the Latin American Biblical Seminary, the national evangelical radio station TIFC ("Lighthouse of the Caribbean"), and the Bible Clinic, as well as the Association of Bible Churches.

The recent boom in evangelicalism in Costa Rica, however, is the direct result of advances by pentecostal churches, mainly Assemblies of God, Church of God, and the Pentecostal Holiness Church, which have been setting up churches since the early 1950s. Besides altering the theological mix in the country, pentecostal growth also has resulted in rival Catholic and more traditional evangelical churches adopting many of the tactics and emotional nature of the pentecostals.

In the 1980s the evangelical movement penetrated the wealthier sectors of Costa Rican society through para-ecclesial organizations. These include Full Gospel Businessmen's Fellowship, Women's Aglow Fellowship, and Ministry to the Student World (MINAMUNDO). Such rightwing U.S.-based evangelical organizations as Campus Crusade for Christ (Alfa y Omega), Globe Missionary Evangelism, Trans-World Missions, Maranatha (New Jerusalem Christian Association), Christian Growth Ministries (publishers of New Wine Magazine), Navigators, and CBN's 700 Club have also recently begun operating in the country, particularly among the middle and upper classes.

Yet with all the evangelical sects to be found in Costa Rica, the country has not been subjected to the massive evangelization campaign by pentecostals and fundamentalists experienced by countries like Guatemala and Honduras. One explanation is that Costa Rica has not suffered the same kind of natural catastrophes and political crises that tend to attract such groups.

Costa Rica has been adopted as a regional center for many evangelical institutions including the Latin American Mission, the evangelical education organization Alfalit, Difusiones Interamericanas (which provides broadcasting services), and the Latin American Evangelical Center for Pastoral Studies (CELEP).

Generally, evangelical churches exert a conservative, pro-U.S. influence in Costa Rican society. In the late 1960s and early 1970s a politically and theologically progressive faction of evangelicals did emerge, forming a base within the Biblical Seminary. But this new dynamism of ecumenism and religious social activism was eventually marginalized by most U.S. missionary societies, and has been largely unsuccessful in gaining a strong following among the evangelical community. A spokesperson for the ecumenical CELEP blames the conservative tenor of Costa Rican evangelicalism on the United States. "Costa Rica is the ideological front for the United States in Central America," she complained. "Fifteen years ago, there used to be an ecumenical movement here, but it was destroyed."

Outside this evangelical movement are numerous other religious groups, most of which have their origin in the United States. These include the Mormons, Jehovah's Witnesses, Theosophical Society, Baha'i, Hari Krishna, and Unification Church.

NGOs and Private Development Organizations

Nongovernmental organizations (NGOs) involved in development, business, and charitable activities proliferated in Costa Rica in the 1980s. Three main factors explain this rapid increase in nonprofit humanitarian and developmental activities: 1) a response to the government's failure to address deteriorating social and economic conditions, 2) the new attention to the NGO sector by AID and other foreign funding agencies, and 3) a tendency to locate regional NGO headquarters in Costa Rica due to its relatively stable and pleasant setting.

NGOs, both local and international, began to emerge in the 1960s. The most prominent local NGO established during the 1960s was the locally based Private Voluntary Federation (FOV), which provides coordination and support mainly for women's charitable organizations. Throughout its history, FOV has received important financial and technical assistance from AID and the U.S.-based Overseas Education Fund (OEF). The widespread availability of government social services and the country's international status as an advanced developing country meant, however, that the NGO sector was quite small before the 1980s.

In the 1970s and early 1980s AID channeled some of its development aid to the government's own community development organization called DINADECO. But later involvement emphasized the privatization of all development assistance. Beginning in 1985 AID began to increase its financial support of and direct involvement in the NGO sector, primarily funding more conservative organizations. Through CINDE, a business NGO created and funded by AID, the agency began to channel funds to a growing number of NGOs. In 1987 CINDE/AID officially established ACORDE as a funding and coordinating organization for NGOs. The AID mission selected the members of ACORDE's board of directors, all of whom were members of the country's business and professional elite with no previous NGO experience.

The formation of ACORDE paralleled similar efforts by AID in other Central American countries to fund and coordinate NGO operations. The Private Agencies Collaborating Together (PACT) representative in Costa Rica confided that AID created ACORDE as a "funding window" for NGOs and that it is now "the only show in town when it comes to getting big bucks for NGO work." According to the PACT representative, "The AID director, Dan Chaij, strongly supported ACORDE because he thought that the AID economic stabilization program for Costa Rica was certain to impoverish some people and that ACORDE could help reduce the social impact of AID policies." ACORDE was created as a "shock absorber."[41]

Excluded from the AID-triggered NGO boom in Costa Rica were a network of highly effective and innovative NGOs that sponsor popular education, community development, and research projects in coordination with the popular organizations. Many of these organizations (such as CENAP, CEDECO, CECADE and ALFORJA) were created in the early 1980s by leftist party intellectuals and ex-militants who, disillusioned with their experience in conventional political arenas, were in search of new forms of political action. They rely mainly on funding from a variety of Canadian and European donors and their efforts are coordinated by the Council of Promotional and Popular Education Centers.

Unlike other Central American countries, where social conditions are more serious, the NGO sectors in Costa Rica do not serve as society's safety net; rather the public sector fills this role. As government-sponsored welfare services are reduced, though, churches and NGOs are gradually moving into social assistance activities. Unfortunately, just as NGOs are forced to redefine their social and political strategies to accommodate structural adjustment, they are also being hit with severe financial cutbacks. Costa Rica, a country that ranks 42nd in the United Nations Human Development Index, is not a priority destination of development funding, and European agencies are slowly withdrawing their support. The coming years will undoubtedly be a period of innovation and adaptation as NGOs struggle to survive in the new political and economic context.

Women and Feminism

In its class character and political agenda, the women's movement in Costa Rica resembles feminism in developed countries. Issues such as sexual preference, battering, job discrimination, and sexual harassment are publicly debated.

Since the 1950s profound social and economic change has forced a redefinition of female lifestyle and identity in Costa Rica. Urbanization and changes in the dominant scheme of production have stimulated a general trend from extended to nuclear families, reducing the average number of children per household from 7 to 3. Due to improvements in public education, women enjoy a literacy rate comparable to men's, around 93 percent, and their participation in university studies is only slightly lower than for their male counterparts.[42] Nevertheless, women tend to concentrate in those disciplines traditionally considered feminine, namely the arts, literature, and education. In general, levels of female education in Costa Rica surpass those in most other parts of Latin America.

Women have also benefited from national improvements in health care. Better nutrition, sanitation infrastructure, and vaccination coverage have all contributed to a decline in female mortality rates that far outpaces other countries in the region. Women's health has also improved due to a fall in fecundity and the growth of state-run maternal-infant care programs. Female life expectancy has increased to 76 years, one of the highest in Latin America.[43]

The Costa Rican government has a history of financing and otherwise encouraging women's organizations. It has supported the FOV, a women's social-service organization, and in 1975 legislated against the sexist use of women's bodies in commercial advertising. Although male officials have often proved initially responsive to women's demands, there has been little real commitment to guarantee women's rights. The measure against sexist advertising, for example, has not been enforced.

As early as 1984 the country had a shelter for battered women, in contrast to the other Central American countries, none of which have established one. The country already has a highly advanced Family Code, which stipulates that a husband and wife have equal rights and equal duties. The code provides equal recourse to divorce for men and women, and allows divorce by mutual consent, thereby avoiding emotionally wrenching court cases.

Other indications of the degree to which women's rights have become a genuine concern among Costa Ricans include the 1989 creation of the office of Women's Defender (later moved to the Public Defender's office) and the 1990 passage of the "Law to Promote the Social Equality of Women" (better known as the "Law of Real Equality"). The latter aims to transform gender equality from legal fiction to actual fact by guaranteeing a woman's right to family patrimony and inheritance—even in the case of free union—maternal leave, and government childcare facilities. The bill's initial draft established quotas of female candidates for the electoral registers of political parties. The article caused such a stir, however, that it was later revised to require the parties simply to encourage female participation in positions of leadership. Four years after their approval, however, few of the above provisions have been obeyed.

Although women's rights are increasingly becoming part of popular social discourse, the overall situation of women has not greatly improved. The continuing economic crisis has apparently resulted in an increase in cases of woman battering, up over 200 percent since 1983. Child abuse rates are also rising. Although men are guilty of most child sexual mistreatment, mothers are largely responsible for physical forms of abuse. Social worker Ana Virginia Quesada explained, "Women are the main perpetrators of physical abuse, possibly as a power assertion along the lines of 'the boss kicks you, you kick the dog'."[44]

Rape has also increased, but convictions have remained few, in part due to a Costa Rican law that requires proof that a rape victim physically resisted her attacker. "In Costa Rica we live with the myth that this is a peaceful society," observed Sara Sharratt, a professor of women's studies at the National University. "We are so busy thinking about no army that we ignore the fact that there is widespread, institutionalized violence against women in this 'peaceful' society."[45]

Since the 1950s women have come to represent 30 percent of Costa Rica's economically active population. Thirty percent of working-age women have jobs, compared to 75 percent of Costa Rican men. Although increased access to income may contribute to women's overall social influence, their participation in the work force has also exposed them to entirely new forms of abuse and discrimination.

Whether due to open salary bias or to their concentration in lower occupational levels, in 1984, women earned only 84 percent of the average male salary. In 1992, the rate of unemployment for women was 5.4 percent compared to 3.5 percent for working-age men. Most female workers concentrate in the service sector, particularly as domestic servants and vendors, however, more and more women are climbing into the technical and professional ranks.[46] Still, women have limited access to managerial and supervisory positions.

The film documentary *Dos Veces Mujer* (Two Times a Woman), produced by a female Costa Rican director, powerfully portrayed the problems faced by women breadwinners. Numerous projects exist to provide productive employment for women living in poor urban areas. Most of these projects, however, are cottage industries in which women sew clothing for substandard wages. One such project sews the clothing used to dress up Barbie dolls for export to the United States.

The growing economic importance of Costa Rican women seems not to have transferred over to the political realm. Despite their contribution to community-based political efforts, women display only minor presence in the institutionalized political system. The number of female deputies in the 57-member Legislative Assembly has barely expanded in the last 40 years, from 3 to 9. Although political opportunities are better in Costa Rica than in most other Latin American countries, women have never occupied more than 15 percent of government offices. In the judicial branch, over 40 percent of judges are women, but they concentrate mainly in the minor courts: 56 percent work in mayoral offices, 27 percent in superior courts, and 5 percent are court magistrates.[47]

Women are similarly underrepresented in the upper ranks of most private social organizations. They make up one third of participants in the cooperative sector but occupy only 15 percent of administrative positions. Only the communal organizations confer greater authority to their female constituency.

Useful as they might be in assessing women's plight in Costa Rica, even official census data are vulnerable to gender biases by underestimating women's importance to society. A 1992 investigation by the Inter-American Institute for Agricultural Cooperation (IICA) boosted the estimated number of women contributing to the rural economy from the official statistic of 6000 to between 60,000 and 80,000 campesinas. Based on this calculation, female involvement in the labor force should be considered much higher than the official government statistic of 8 percent. Such statistical invisibility has resulted in women's near absolute exclusion from agricultural sector policies, including access to land, state bank credit, and training programs sponsored by the Ministry of Agriculture and Animal Husbandry.[48] In recent years, only 27 percent of women who solicited land qualified as beneficiaries, while 61 percent of men were registered.

For the last two decades, sterilization has been the second most common form of birth control for women. According to the Ministry of Health, 25 percent of Costa Rican women are sterile. Yet sterilization is illegal; and its legalization as a woman's choice has been strongly opposed by the Catholic Church, which says that legalized sterilization would be the first step toward legalized abortion.

Birth control in Costa Rica is a nationalistic and feminist issue, as well as a religious one. Many critics say that foreign agencies like AID and Planned Parenthood are undermining the sovereignty and dignity of Costa Ricans with their birth control campaigns. They point out that many Costa Rican women were sterilized without their consent in the 1950s. Costa Rican feminists, however, assert that sterilization, like other forms of birth control, is their right. As a Costa Rican feminist publication stated: "Women don't choose sterilization just because they are ignorant or are forced without consent. Social problems such as lack of employment, education, decent housing, medical services, and safe, secure contraception are decisive factors."[49]

The decrease in social services and worsening economic conditions for the poor may account for the alarming incidence of adolescent mothers in recent years. Public health officials estimate that every 52 seconds a teenaged girl gives birth. One-fourth of all Costa Rican women have their first child between 15 and 18 years of age, and 40 percent of the female adolescent population is not in school. One-fifth of these teenagers work as maids. These statistics indicate that previous advances in education and equal opportunity won by Costa Rican women may now be reversed by the new economic and political climate.[50]

Indigenous Communities

Costa Rica is largely a *mestizo* society but with lighter skin tones than those of other Central American countries—a trait explained by the historical absence of a widespread native population. Today, there are approximately thirty thousand indigenous people in the country (less than 1 percent of Costa Rica's population of 3.2 million), most of whom live within the twenty-two reserves established by the government. The majority of Costa Rica's indigenous population occupies isolated stretches of jungle near the Panamanian border, although other reserves are found further north along the Pacific Coast. As in other parts of tropical America, the surviving indigenous groups of Costa Rica have transformed from a tribal to a peasant society.[51]

Not only are these Costa Rican natives isolated from the dominant society, they are isolated from each other, both by their geographical obstacles and by their own cultural differences. Eight different communities exist within the small indigenous population, although only six native languages have survived the last five hundred years of colonization.

Costa Rica boasts a progressive policy regarding its native peoples. In 1977 the government passed the Indigenous Bill establishing the right of natives to land reserves and authorizing measures to preserve native culture and language. Not simply paperwork, the bill has resulted in government programs to promote native culture and to introduce bilingual education for native students. But numerous indigenous community leaders complain that the government has not adequately protected indigenous land rights and treats the native people solely as a tourist attraction. As Baldomero Torres, a member of the Cabagra community, commented, "We don't want to be treated as animals in a zoo, but we do need help to improve our poor living conditions."

While the government is given much credit for promoting native culture, it gets few good marks when it comes to preserving indigenous land rights. On many reserves, the majority of land has fallen into the hands of "white" Costa Ricans. Nonindigenous cattle ranchers and farmers have seized and fenced native land with impunity. Natives living in the extensive Talamanca Reserve, which straddles the border with Panama, are also threatened by increasing land speculation, mining, and petroleum exploration. The Cabécar and Bribri communities, the largest ethnic groups in the country, who make their homes in the Talamanca mountains, are widely scattered in migratory family units and have not formed the kind of political and social organizations that could better protect their lands and their culture against encroaching outside interests.[52] The Indigenous Bill originally required that private interests obtain permits for mining exploitation in the reserves from an organization representing native interests, the National Commission of Indian Issues (CONAI). The 1982 Mining Code, however, transferred this authority to the Legislative Assembly, thus depriving native people of any direct control over the use of mining resources on their own lands.

The economic and political marginalization of indigenous communities in Costa Rica differs little from the sufferings of indigenous populations elsewhere in Central America. Communities are plagued by an alarming lack of transportation, communications, and public services infrastructure. Educational facilities only provide schooling to the fourth grade and 50 percent of the indigenous population is illiterate.[53] The Commission for the Defense of Human Rights in Central America (CODEHUCA) estimates that well over half of houses and latrines in indigenous communities are in total disrepair. It asserts that most native deaths could be avoided with adequate sanitation facilities and blame the state's abandonment of indigenous reserves for exceedingly high incidences of diarrhea, bronchitis, anemia, chicken pox, measles, tuberculosis, and malaria. Adding insult to injury, deforestation and agricultural pesticides have contributed to the disappearance of many local medicinal plants. Of every one thousand infants born in the indigenous region of Chirripó, forty-four die, compared to the national average of fourteen.[54]

The relegation of Costa Rica's native population to second-class status is perhaps best illustrated by the fact that indigenous peoples were not granted citizenship and did not receive personal identification cards until 1992. Indians were allowed to vote for the first time in the 1994 elections.

Economic development is an issue that now confronts the indigenous communities of Costa Rica. At a time when many are taking steps to preserve their culture from further deterioration, they are also being faced with decisions about how best to promote their economic interests. A case in point is a controversy that has surfaced in

Talamanca. Opposition has arisen there to the development projects of the AID-financed New Alchemists Association (ANAI), whose objective is to transform the agricultural practices of peasant farmers, chiefly by introducing the production of nontraditional crops. One indigenous group called the Cultural Committee charged that ANAI representatives are foreigners who "come to teach us how to use medicinal plants which they cannot have known before they arrived here." The committee also noted, "We have thousands of years of experience of living based on agriculture, and we know much better which are appropriate soils to plant in, as well as the moon cycles to coordinate the planting." But other indigenous communities in Talamanca and elsewhere stress economic development over cultural traditions.[55]

As isolated as most Costa Rican indigenous communities may be, they have been reached by the dominant culture of the country. While they may live without electricity and running water, Costa Rican natives do live in a culture of soft drinks and junk food, and battery-powered TVs are commonly found on the reserves.

Refugees and Migrants

Over the last couple decades, Costa Rica has served as a haven for Latin American political exiles. But it was not until the late 1970s, when thousands of Nicaraguans crossed the border to escape growing repression unleashed by Somoza, that Costa Rica gained its present status as host to large concentrations of Central American refugees. Most of these Nicaraguans returned to their home country after the Sandinistas' victory over Somoza in 1979, but their numbers were soon replaced by Salvadorans fleeing the escalating violence in that country. With the heating up of the contra war and later as economic conditions worsened in Nicaragua, tens of thousands of Nicaraguans once again sought refuge in Costa Rica.

The massive influx of Nicaraguans, most of them poor, uneducated rural dwellers, sparked considerable resentment among Costa Ricans and soon became a source of tension between the two countries. Nicaraguans were blamed for the reappearance of diseases that long ago had been eradicated, as well as for growing rates of crime and violence. The Nicaraguan government refused to take full responsibility for the migrant dilemma, pointing out that, for years, Costa Rican radio stations broadcast messages into Nicaragua encouraging people to leave the country and join the contra resistance.

Through most of the 1980s immigration policy granted legal residence only to migrants who qualified for political refugee status. Refugees were loosely consolidated in encampments and were eligible for government identification cards that permitted employment in jobs that would not displace Costa Rican workers. Normally refugees could find temporary work in banana plantations and other low-paying, manual labor positions.

In late 1988 a joint accord between Costa Rica and Nicaragua created dual border patrols and instituted the voluntary repatriation of any Nicaraguans who did not qualify as political refugees. Over a four year period some 22,000 Nicaraguans and 1,000 Salvadorans were returned to their countries of origin, culminating in the closing of the refugee camps in May of 1994.[56]

In 1989 the International Conference on Central American Refugees (CIREFCA), a derivative of the Esquipulas II Accords, was held in Guatemala to formulate a plan of action regarding the region's refugee and migrant problems. Through regional negotiations CIREFCA was established as a permanent organization to coordinate the activities of Central American governments, NGOs, the Office of the United Nations High Commissioner for Refugees (UNHCR), and other international agencies. An important outcome of the meeting was the reconceptualization of migration not as a temporary and emergency condition, but as a process that is integrally related to the processes of political and economic development in Central America.

Costa Rica's policy on immigration changed again in 1992 when President Rafael Calderón enacted an executive decree that issued permanent and temporary residence to recognized refugees and undocumented migrants. In one year the government granted approximately 8,800 residence permits. Whether due to fear or ignorance, however, an estimated 15,000 refugees and an estimated 80,000 other migrants failed to take advantage of the new program. In recent years the government has also launched programs in the impoverished rural and peri-urban areas where migrants concentrate. These progams aim to expand economic opportunities, improve local infrastructure, and integrate the displaced communities into the surrounding population.[57]

The immigration dilemma promises to get stickier for Costa Rican authorities in the coming years. Every day an estimated 400 Nicaraguans enter the country illegally, adding to the nearly half million Nicaraguans residing in the country already.[58] In the latter half of 1994 the Ministry of the Interior strengthened its efforts to control unauthorized entrance and deported some 12,000 undocumented Nicaraguans. Although Interior Ministry officials acknowledge the benefits of Nicaraguan labor to Costa Rican agroindustry, they contend that immigrants are a source of rising crime and constitute a significant health risk. Many immigrants are reputed to suffer from dengue, tuberculosis, and malaria. Nevertheless the Nicaraguan press has been quick to point out inconsistencies in Costa Ricans' views on immigration: even as they applauded efforts to repatriate Nicaraguans, Costa Ricans were condemning the recent passage of Proposition 187 as discriminatory toward Central American residents in California.

Despite popular resentment toward Nicaraguan immigrants, the Costa Rican government has recently loosened northern border restraints to compensate for national labor shortages in the coffee, sugar, and banana industries. The government shares agreements with Nicaragua and local businesses to facilitate the transfer of labor; companies are only asked to return workers to their countries once their period of work is concluded, and to abide by the same labor norms that apply to the domestic work force. In May of 1994 some 1,000 workers from the transnational banana company Geest Caribbean Americas Ltd. held a strike demanding better wages and labor rights for undocumented Nicaraguan laborers. The immigrants maintained that, because of their legal status, they are denied union participation, their legal right to job benefits, and that they are paid lower salaries than their Costa Rican counterparts. The vulnerability of immigrant labor poses major problems for unions seeking to organize workers in the banana industry.

Part 5

Environment

© Steven Rubin/Impact Visuals

Environment

Environmentalism in Costa Rica is marked by contradiction. On the one hand, the country enjoys international recognition for its well-developed system of national parks and forest reserves. On the other, Costa Rica's ecological integrity is slowly dissolving in the face of rapid deforestation, extensive soil erosion, indiscriminate pesticide use, and uncontrolled dumping of industrial wastes. Surprisingly, Costa Rica suffers from one of the highest rates of forest loss in the world.[1] The irony is not wasted upon environmental policymakers, who observe that Costa Rica's development model is slowly degrading the very resource base it depends so heavily upon.

Destruction of Natural Resources

The pace of environmental destruction in Costa Rica accelerated dramatically in the early 1950s as the shift from a small-scale agricultural economy to industrial and export-oriented forms of production intensified land use and drove landless rural dwellers into urban centers.[2] In contrast with the self-sustaining agricultural practices of Costa Rica's once-dominant peasant population, contemporary agroindustry makes less efficient use of the natural resources it exploits. Fully forty percent of the organic matter collected in commercial banana harvests and 70 percent of products from coffee are wasted, often dumped into rivers where they contribute most of the country's water pollutants. Environmentalists also point out that banana and coffee production generate valuable byproducts—modified starches, pectin, caffeine, and pharmaceutical derivatives—that are fully within the technological capacity of these industries to exploit.[3]

Agroindustrial inefficiencies, however, are overshadowed by the other ecological dilemmas facing Costa Rica. According to a study by the Ministry of Natural Resources, Energy, and Mines (MIRENEM),

Figure 5a
Deforestation in Costa Rica

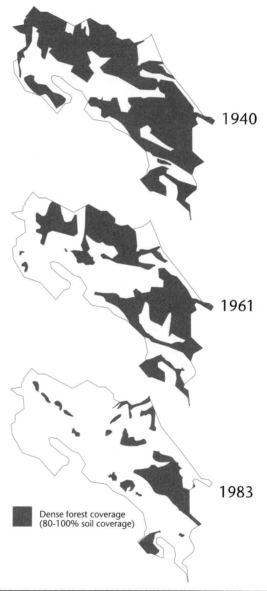

1940

1961

1983

Dense forest coverage
(80-100% soil coverage)

SOURCE: Anabelle Porras and Beatriz Villareal, *Deforestacion en Costa Rica* (San José: Editorial Costa Rica, 1986), p. 23.

"Land use conflicts constitute the gravest environmental problem of all in Costa Rica."[4] Cattle grazing is a principal source of dispute in this regard. The rapid expansion of the cattle industry through the 1960s and 1970s resulted in the destruction—primarily by burning—of vast expanses of woodlands. An estimated 90 percent of the forests felled during that period are forever lost. The transition also had significant repercussions for social and economic development because it withdrew extensive areas of land from agricultural production and offered little employment by way of compensation. Although only 8 percent of Costa Rica's lands are apt for cattle grazing, pasture currently covers 44 percent of the national territory.

There was a time when two-thirds of Costa Rica's surface area was blanketed in tropical forest; today the country has lost more than three-quarters of its original woodlands.[5] Although sources vary widely, MIRENEM estimates that the rate of deforestation went from 36,000 hectares annually in the 1950s to 50,000 hectares per year in the 1970s and mid-1980s.[6] Despite differences in deforestation estimates, sources agree that until 1987 Costa Rican forests were disappearing at a faster rate than anywhere else in Central America—faster, in fact, than most countries throughout the world. Between 1983 and 1990 Costa Rica's forest reserves fell by 26 percent.[7] A 1987 satellite study found that only 250,000 hectares of commercially productive forest remained to Costa Rica. Many predict that by the turn of the century the country will be forced to import timber (Figure 5a).

Among the most important causes of deforestation in Costa Rica are that trees are removed with no formal plan for replacement and that legislators view forests more as obstacles to development than as valuable, potentially sustainable resources. With the expansion of commercial cattle grazing and banana and coffee production, more and more landless rural dwellers have been forced to invade forested areas. Indeed, the state itself has encouraged campesinos to colonize frontier zones, contributing further to the extent of deforestation. The General Forestry Office (DGF) estimates that between 1989 and 1991 illegal tree cutting accounted for 80 percent of forest losses.[8]

Deforestation and inappropriate land use also produce high rates of soil erosion, deteriorating watersheds, and declining water levels in rivers throughout the country. An estimated 42 percent of all soils in Costa Rica show traces of severe erosion. The country loses about 725 million tons of topsoil to wind-blown erosion and water runoff each year, of which 83 percent (600 million tons) comes from areas dedicated to pasture.[9] At least half of drainage basins are overexploited by agriculture and grazing, and some areas even suffer incipient desertification. Watershed deterioration presents a particularly serious threat to the country's hydroelectric system, which produces most of the country's electric power. Reservoirs are silting up at a rapid rate, costing the hydroelectric system hundreds of millions of dollars in lost revenues.

Inappropriate land use is not just about losing forests or water resources but also involves the disappearance of natural habitats, flora, and fauna. Despite its small size (51,000 km^2), Costa Rica has one of the highest levels of biological diversity in the world, including an estimated ten to twelve thousand different plant species and 1,450 species of birds, mammals, and other vertebrate life. By the late 1980s environmental degradation and hunting threatened the extinction of 103 varieties of wild animals (72 bird, 24 mammal, 4 reptile, and 3 amphibian species) as well as 45 species of trees.[10]

The unplanned growth of towns and cities creates another land-use dilemma. In the last quarter-century, urban sprawl has taken over the Central Valley, spreading concrete over the country's most fertile region—an agricultural heartland distinguished by rich volcanic soil and low-relief terrain. The San José metropolis now covers about 4 percent of the national territory and holds more than 50 percent of the population. Spreading out from San José, uncontrolled urban growth is consuming vegetable and dairy farms. If growth rates continue, this area could house up to 1.8 million people by the year 2000, and in the process destroy some of the richest coffee-producing land in the world. Streams that intersect this exploding metropolis are already clogged with trash and wastes.

Intensive and indiscriminate use of insecticides, herbicides, and other agricultural chemicals adds to the growing list of environmental threats confronting Costa Rica's inhabitants. Pesticide abuse was previously concentrated in the traditional agroexport crops like bananas and sugar. Yet with a new focus on nontraditional exports, the major threat lies in uncontrolled spraying by producers of vegetables and flowers. Agricultural chemicals have all but exterminated armadillos, fish, and crocodiles along the Tempisque River. Cancers, physical deformities, and sterility in human populations have also been traced to pesticides. Every year more than 6 percent of Costa Rican banana workers present claims with the National Institute of Securities (INS) for labor incidents involving pesticides—the highest incidence of recorded intoxications in the world.[11] Since the country has no government agency—although one has been proposed—that monitors food products for harmful chemicals, even the general populace is not safe from chemical contamination.

Although pesticides may be the most toxic source of water pollutant, agroindustrial discharge contributes the highest volume of contaminants. Organic matter left over from coffee and sugar processing in the Central Valley contributes 80 percent of agricultural effluents, mostly in the Big Tárcoles River, which drains into the Gulf of Nicoya. The coffee industry alone is considered the most important source of water contamination in the country. The deteriorating quality of river water spurs an increasing reliance on more costly subterranean water sources.[12]

Solid waste disposal has also reached problematic proportions, particularly in Costa Rica's urban centers. According to the Neotropic Foundation, over half of material refuse goes uncollected and untreated and often winds up in nearby rivers.[13] Many of Costa Rica's urban landfills are at the limit of their capacity, like the Río Azul dump, which receives most of San José's waste. The government is developing alternative ways to treat and store refuse.

Protection and Conservation of the Natural Environment

Despite progressive ecological deterioration, Costa Rica has the reputation among its Central American neighbors for having taken the boldest steps to protect the environment. The government's efforts to create an extensive system of protected natural areas stand at the center of the country's commitment to environmental conservation. In fact almost one-quarter of Costa Rica's territory is devoted to national parks, forest reserves, indigenous reservations, and wildlife refuges. These areas contain nearly all of the wild species found in the country, and span the majority of its ecosystems.[14] Although large sections of the forest reserves and wildlife refuges lie on private land, all protected areas fall under state inspection.

Focus on Costa Rica by such international environmental organizations as the World Wildlife Fund and the Nature Conservancy has contributed to the country's reputation for environmental concern. It has also increased the presence in Costa Rica of an influential community of foreign-born environmentalists, notably the Quakers and their sponsorship of the Monteverde reserve. Credit for the country's national park program must also go to Olof Wessberg and Karen Morgensen, who, from their home in the remote Nicoya Peninsula, began pushing for a national park system in the 1960s.[15]

International conservation organizations have joined Costa Rica's efforts to establish a large national park system through what has been called the Debt-for-Nature Swap program. Organizations like the Nature Conservancy, the World Wildlife Fund, and the World Fund for Flora and Fauna purchase some of the nation's external debt from foreign banks, usually at less than 20 percent of face value. The government's Central Bank then buys this debt with short-term government bonds, with the stipulation that the funds be used for conservation. More than $40 million has been invested in this innovative manner of debt settlement.

Some critics charge that the Debt-for-Nature Swap fuels inflationary tendencies while reducing pressure for debt restructuring. National sovereignty is also at stake in a program that allows international organizations to make resource planning decisions rightfully made by governments themselves. For the most part, though, the debt swaps have been widely applauded as a way to stop the continued destruction of the environment—although the small scale of the financial agreements does not make them a real alternative to serious debt restructuring.

The integration of peasants (and communities living within or on the borders of national parks) into park planning and development has been another trend that distinguishes environmental protection in Costa Rica. According to the minister of natural resources, this "mixed management" approach involves "managing buffer zones as integral to the protected area, teaching rural people agroforestry, and training them as tourist guides." Unfortunately some campesino organizations are less than enthusiastic about the way integrated development has played out. They complain that state officials often place the forest's survival above their own well-being, and prohibit landowners from using resources contained in their own plantations.

The national park system is just one sign of developing environmental consciousness in Costa Rica. The cultural shift can also be gauged by the addition of 28 new laws between 1965 and 1985 protecting the country's lands, waters, and forests and preserving its genetic diversity. In 1986 the Ministry of Industry, Energy, and Mines was transformed into the Ministry of Natural Resources, Energy, and Mines and assigned the new mission of regulating natural resource use. With the creation of the National Institute of Biodiversity (IN-BIO), the government now monitors the state of the country's rarest animal and plant species. Some have labeled it the most important center for the study of tropical ecology in the world.

Although the environmental movement achieved significant gains in the 1980s and early 1990s, laws and good intentions have fallen short of effective conservation. Legally established wildlands occupy a major chunk of the country's land base but less than one-half of this area is adequately protected. Reserve perimeters are under constant threat by landless campesinos and land speculators. Wealthy individuals with lumber and cattle interests are known to pay second parties to invade and settle protected areas as a way of extending grazing and timber extraction zones. One forest preserve in particular, Osa National Park, has succumbed to major stream and watershed damage on the part of gold miners.

Not all parks in Costa Rica are government-owned. Some are managed privately, and cost as much as $75 a day to enjoy. This privatization of nature worries some Costa Rican environmentalists, who are also concerned about the explosion of an ecotourism industry largely controlled by foreigners. In the late 1980s there was a 50 percent increase in businesses catering to such avocations as bird watching and white-water rafting. The government, which has encouraged these new entrepreneurs, has begun to see the environment in terms of its ability to generate foreign exchange from international tourists.

In fact, ecotourism may be sowing the seeds of its own destruction. Although tourists come to the country to share in its natural richness, they often stay in hotels and tourist complexes that make minimal effort to ease their impact on the surrounding ecology. The number of visitors to the national parks and preserves similarly takes its toll on trails and vegetation. In response, the government has taken measures to limit access to protected areas according to the capacity of these environments to absorb impact. Another proposal is for the state to grant certificates of environmental protection that hotels could display as evidence that tourists will not contribute to ecological degradation by staying in their facilities.

In addition to the national park system, environmentalism manifests itself in efforts to reforest the Costa Rican countryside. MIRENEM calculates that between 1970 and 1980 forested land increased by an average of 1,300 hectares per year. Over three-quarters of this acreage was reforested with state assistance in the form of fiscal incentives and soft credit. Early on in the government's reforestation campaign only a scattering of large companies cashed in on government benefits. A growing proportion of small- and middle-holding farmers have been joining the ranks, however, perhaps signaling the development of a more forest-conscious culture in rural areas.

Another encouraging sign is the emergence of community environmental initiatives. Examples include the Guapiles neighborhood association's concern with deforestation, the struggle by the Desamparados community to stop coffee-processing plants from dumping wastes in nearby rivers, and the growing interest among small farmers in organic vegetable production. An ever-present pitfall for all grassroots initiatives, however, is cooptation by the government or international institutions. The militancy and effectiveness of a leading environmental organization, ASCONA, was severely undermined by its association with the PLN and AID, for example.[16]

In October of 1994 the Central American presidents met in Managua, Nicaragua, to sign on to a cooperative strategy for regional development called the Alliance for Sustainable Development. The document sets forth an agenda promoting democratization, the fight against poverty, and sustainable growth founded in respect for cultural, social, and environmental development. Despite its broad parameters, the alliance is decidedly ecological in focus, calling for increased vigilance regarding endangered species and protected areas. As an addendum to the agreement, the presidents endorsed the Declaration of Masaya Volcano, which lays out specific terms for "the conservation and management of water resources, the gradual elimination of leaded gasoline, and the classification and identification of the most depleted soils" in the region. The meeting in Masaya Volcano National Park also elicited commitments to the appropriate use of natural resources and to regulating pollution both through programs of environmental education and by the creation of an "environment fund."

Although the Alliance for Sustainable Development seems to be a step in the right direction, environmentalists are profoundly skeptical that the Central American governments will stick to their conservationist commitments when faced with economic pressures from mining, ranching, chemical, and logging interests to ease restrictions. The fact that environmental groups and journalists were largely excluded from the summit did not calm worries in this regard.

On an international scale, another novel environmental initiative to emerge in recent years proposes that industrialized nations pay underdeveloped countries for the service that their forests perform in absorbing industrial carbon dioxide emissions. The United States and Costa Rica took the first steps in this direction when they signed the "Bilateral Agreement of Cooperation for Sustainable Development and Implementation" during the 1994 United Nations Convention on Climatic Changes. A principal aim of the accord is to promote U.S. investment in the massive reforestation of Costa Rica to compensate for environmental contamination produced by U.S. industry. Promising as this development may be, the Figueres administration has given no evidence that it can reconcile its professed commitment to "development in harmony with nature" with the new model of economic development, whose extensive agroexport component depends on cheap labor and land.

Part 6

Central American Integration, Free Trade Treaties, and Globalization

© Sean Sprague/Impact Visuals

Early Initiatives for Regional Integration

In 1960 five Central American nations—Guatemala, El Salvador, Honduras, Nicaragua, and Costa Rica—signed the treaty of Central American Economic Integration, marking the beginning of region's experience in economic integration. The treaty established the foundation for the Central American Common Market (CACM), a system of common tariffs that generated intense growth in regional commerce rooted in programs of import substitution industrialization. The CACM stimulated Costa Rican industry by virtually eliminating tariffs on goods moving within Central America and by escalating tariffs on imports from outside the region (with the exception of capital goods and raw material required by industry). The high growth rates that the Central American countries experienced during the 1960s and 1970s have led analysts to label the CACM as the most successful attempt at regional integration in Latin American history.[1] Two years after the signing of the economic integration treaty and the creation of the CACM, the five Central American countries signed another accord that established the Organization of Central American States (ODECA) as the institution to oversee the institutional framework of economic integration.

Toward the end of the 1970s the CACM entered a phase of severe contraction and economic paralyzation. The causes for this were manifold: the stagnation of the import substitution industrialization model, economic tensions between lesser and more-developed countries in the region, political and military crises in Guatemala, El Salvador, and the Sandinista revolution in Nicaragua, which dramatically altered the norms of diplomatic relations in the region. Recognizing it was time for change, the Central American countries one by one redefined their involvement in the regional agreements that resulted from the treaty of Central American Economic Integration. As regional diplomacy collapsed, the Central American forums that had sustained the CACM lost their meaning.[2]

Negotiations surrounding the Esquipulas Peace Accords opened a new chapter of foreign diplomacy in Central America. Signed by the region's presidents in 1987, the peace plan began to dispel concerns within the international donor community that political and military threats rendered impossible most regional economic development efforts with the region. In the wake of the Esquipulas meeting, regional summits bringing together Central America's presidents resulted in new plans for regional cooperation. Unlike the internally-focused development vision of the CACM, this new spurt of interest in regional integration was more outward-looking. Each nation recognized the need to present a unified regional front in extraregional negotiations regarding free trade and other aspects of global economic integration. Regional cooperation that had been sparked by a common desire to bring peace to Central America has come to concentrate mostly on economic issues.[3]

Beginning in 1990 with the electoral defeat of the Sandinistas, the Central American presidents began to shift regional diplomacy from the priorities of regional security and peace established in the Esquipulas Accord to issues of economic development and growth. In the 1990 Antigua Summit (also known as the Central American Economic Summit) country leaders signed on to the Central American Plan for Economic Action (PAECA), which proposed a series of mechanisms to normalize trade.

An outward-looking strategy for development, PAECA launched a regional program aimed at adapting the integration process to the new strategies of foreign trade and modernization.[4] The plan proposed to convert the region into a vast free trade area and to formulate a united platform from which the Central American nations could negotiate in the world market. Following the 1990 Antigua summit, the Central American countries have tended to enter into multilateral negotiations as a trade bloc, as demonstrated by the "San José Dialogues" between Central America and the European Union (EU).

In light of the region's new structure of economic integration, the Central American presidents in 1991 endorsed the Tegucigalpa Protocol and created the System of Central American Integration (SICA). The charter officially added Panama to the process of regional integration begun by the other five countries that formed the CACM. In 1993 country leaders signed the Protocol to the treaty of Central American Economic Integration to put forth the principles and procedures that would guide the new Central American integration. In addition to these two protocols, a series of regional forums under SICA have also issued agreements, resolutions, and rules and directorates to fine tune the process of regional cooperation.[5]

For the most part, SICA coordinates economic policies between countries of the region both by reducing internal tariffs and nontariff barriers to trade and by establishing a common external tariff on imports and a common customs regime. It also addresses such common trade issues as the rules of origin, dumping, compensatory tariffs, and safeguard clauses. In addition, SICA institutes policies to control rates of exchange, prices, rates of interest, and government participation in marketing, technical assistance, and land distribution. The underlying purpose of SICA is to establish a general framework and clear rules for regional economic activity. It aims, thereby, to minimize problems arising from the distribution of the costs and benefits of this trade and to ensure that the incentives offered to productive sectors are roughly equal. These conditions are seen as prerequisites to the development of a regional free trade zone and to the ability to negotiate in a unified way with countries outside the region.

The regional coordination of trade policies has been favored by the participation of the Central American countries in the General Agreement on Trade and Tariffs (GATT), which seeks to eliminate restrictions on free trade and apply rules on customs valorization, dumping, and subsidies. Perhaps the greatest facilitators of all to integration, however, are the programs of structural adjustment promoted by international financing organizations that have been active in the region since the 1980s. As Costa Rican economist Alvaro López observed, "Central America is nothing more than the resonance box for what happens at the level of each Central American country."[6]

One of the novelties of the Tegucigalpa Protocol is that it makes room for broad participation from civil society in the decisionmaking processes affecting integration. The Central American presidents created the Consultive Commission, composed of business, labor, and academic leaders, as an advisory body to the secretary general of SICA.[7]

In addition to the Consultive Commission, there exists a behind-the-scenes movement promoting nongovernmental participation in regional and extraregional cooperation that some have called the "real integration."[8] According to proponents of "real integration," solidarity among the Central American populations, resulting from their common experiences of war and natural disaster, can serve as a foundation for increased regional cooperation. They advocate the creation of regional business, farmer, and nongovernmental organizations to guide this people- and business-centered integration.[9]

An unprecedented phenomenon in the region is that campesinos, workers, and small-business owners have recently been coming together to form these kinds of regional organizations. The last few years have seen the emergence of the Association of Central American Campesino Organizations for Cooperation and Development (ASOCODE), Central American Federation of Communal Organizations (FCOC), and the the Central American Worker Network (CO-CENTRA)—organizations created to develop common strategies and campaigns for struggle in the region.

The Central American Committee of Intersectorial Cooperation (CACI) has also taken advantage of the space provided by the presidential summits for civil society in regional integration. It claims to be the representative of social cooperation efforts in the region. The CACI is led by the Federation of Private Entities in Central America and Panamá (FEDEPRICAP), an umbrella organization for the Central American business sector that draws on strong participation from the *solidarista* organizations. Frustrated by the CACI's claim to be the sole voice of civil society, as well as by its cooption by the business sector, the regional popular organizations opted to create their own organization to participate in the process of integration. The Civil Initiative for Central American Integration (ICIC) was formed in 1993 with the objective of promoting what the member organizations describe as "integration from below."

Efforts to push forward a process of political integration at a regional level date back to the proposals of the Esquipulas Peace Accords. Not all Central American countries support expanded regional political integration, however, and it appears that the prospects of cooperation at the political level are not as hopeful as those that are unfolding at the economic level. In 1991 three countries—Guatemala, Honduras, and El Salvador—endorsed regional initiatives to create the Central American Parliament (PARLACEN).[10] Not only has PARLACEN failed to incorporate all of the region's countries, but its role in a more integrated Central America is still subject to much debate. In the Tegucigalpa Protocol the PARLACEN was described as an "organization of planning, analysis, and recommendation," but there is much controversy about what this really means.[11]

Throughout Central America there is a recognition that regional integration should extend beyond strictly political and economic initiatives. Regional meetings to formulate a plan for Central American social integration are planned for February 1995. Similarly, regional leaders are discussing proposals to combine efforts in the areas of infrastructure (ports and roads), services (electricity and other forms of energy), and telecommunications (including the introduction of fiberoptics).

Contemporary Efforts at Central American Integration

Costa Rica has taken an active role in negotiations surrounding the new integrationist order in regional economics. Costa Rica's interests in regional cooperation are motivated as much by its desire for easier access to Central American markets as by the need to join the Central America union if it is to be included in extraregional trade initiatives and development plans.

Raised in the protective environment of the Central American Common Market, Costa Rican industry has long depended on regional outlets for its products. Even today Central America constitutes the third most important destination for Costa Rican exports, especially medicines, containers, bread products, and milk. Despite the contraction of regional trade that occurred in the 1980s, Costa Rican industrialists have been at the forefront of domestic support for regional economic integration.

Stagnation in regional commerce during the 1980s did not occur without some enduring consequences. Partly encouraged by economic policies promoting nontraditional export production, the crisis compelled industrialists to seek new markets outside of the region. Little by little the character of the industrial sector and the destinations of its exports changed. Between 1980 and 1991 the proportion of industrial goods sent to Central America dropped from 72 percent to 32 percent.[12]

The most recent initiative to diversify export markets involves Costa Rica's free trade treaty with Mexico. Initiated in 1995, the agreement promises the nation's industries a market of 90 million new consumers. Also taking effect in 1995 are accords stemming from Costa Rica's entrance into the multilateral trade agreement, GATT. Costa Rica's integration into the global market may be promoted further by developing plans for a much-touted continental free trade zone in the American Hemisphere.

On other fronts, Costa Rica has made it clear that it will not participate in the politically-oriented PARLACEN. Although the government has cited concerns of aligning itself with authoritarian regimes (due to their affiliation with armed forces) in the region, it seems that the most objectionable aspects of PARLACEN are its cost and the loss of political sovereignty that incorporation would represent. The election of parliamentary representatives in PARLACEN countries aroused little interest in Costa Rican political circles, making Costa Rica's inclusion in the parliament even less likely: politicians will not want to commit themselves to an unpopular issue like political integration once national election time draws near. Costa Ricans perceive that few advantages are to be gained from PARLACEN and sentiments of regional solidarity are few and far between. Echoing the public's predilections, Foreign Commerce Minister Roberto Rojas concluded that "it is evident that Costa Rica is not interested in political integration."[13]

Costa Rica's resistance to PARLACEN has demonstrated the limits of regional integration plans. Other proposals to unify the region by opening national borders to the free flow of labor and goods, eliminating national customs, and creating a regional currency have also been soundly rejected. Costa Rican labor leaders argue that unrestricted borders would mean the influx of cheap, foreign labor and the depression of wages. Indeed, some analysts estimate that nearly one million Central Americans would flood into Costa Rica in pursuit of jobs. There is a growing belief among political leaders that any attempt to push integrationist measures beyond strictly economic agreements could have severe consequences for the party in power. As Roberto Rojas observed, "The government that makes that decision [to open borders] would commit political suicide."[14]

There is little chance that Costa Rica will agree to regional currency integration or unifying customs procedures. A significant proportion of the government's tax income comes from foreign trade. Prior to any reorganization of customs processes, the state would have to reform its tax structure to reduce its dependence on customs incomes—an unlikely prospect.

Although Costa Ricans generally regard expanded regional economic integration as positive, there is common agreement that Costa Rica should continue to protect economic sectors that would be threatened by unregulated free trade. As Costa Rica's experience with black-market Nicaraguan agricultural goods has already demonstrated, removing border restrictions would mean competition for local farmers with products from countries where production costs are much lower.

During the Calderón administration, trade officials supported a gradualist approach to integration, permitting countries to proceed at their own pace, without having to accept the entire packet of economic integration as a precondition to participation. This position emerged in response to pressures by the other Central American countries for Costa Rica to immerse itself more fully in the processes of integration. After having led integrationist efforts in the early years of the CACM, Costa Rica found itself at the rear of the pack in the 1990s. Instead of exploring new ways to push regional integration forward, Costa Rica began to look outside the region, establishing free trade treaties with Mexico and Colombia.

By the end of the Calderón administration, regional tensions arising from Costa Rica's ambivalence over integration had diminished. There was increasing recognition among country leaders that Central American integration would only be successful if each country were free to proceed at its own pace according to its particular circumstances. By the time José María Figueres took office in 1994, relations between Costa Rica and the other Central American nations had noticeably improved.

During his first year in office, Figueres exhibited much greater interest in integration than his political predecessor, insisting that Costa Rica negotiate with countries outside the region only through the Central America trade bloc. Many business and political leaders were disturbed by Figueres' less-than-nationalistic approach to regional trade. Even if they acknowledged that Central American integration promised new opportunities for foreign commerce, they insisted that national economic priorities, particularly the free trade agreement with Mexico, should not be sacrificed in the pursuit of regional unity. The Coalition of Initiatives for Development (CINDE) echoed the sentiments of many within the business community: "The Central America market should not be constituted as a brake to legitimate aspirations for the complete integration of our nation with international commerce. Our negotiations with Mexico have not created a disadvantage for other countries in the region. In any case, more than the interest in other countries, our own interest should be foremost in our minds."[15] Such rhetoric and attitudes imposed significant constraints on Figueres' ability to assume a leading role in efforts to unite the region on levels both economic and political.

Nonetheless, José Figueres discovered an attractive and relatively noncontentious issue from which to maintain his political initiative: environmental conservation. With the 1994 Central American Ecological Summit for Sustainable Development he launched an aggressive campaign to combine economic growth with natural resource conservation. The accord established a timeline for implementing regional measures to support biodiversity, environmental impact analyses, forest resources, alternative energy forms, and pollution control.[16] Country leaders also proposed frameworks for cooperative action in human development, the struggle against poverty, and the strengthening of democratic institutions. An important thrust of Figueres' environmental strategy is to attract extraregional partners who can contribute financing for the Alliance's programs through the Central American Environmental Fund.

Globalization and Free Trade Treaties

In addition to participating in the process of Central American integration, Costa Rica has initiated various bilateral negotiations outside of the region. The most important of these in recent years has been the Free Trade Treaty (TLC) with Mexico, a deal that took three years to sign and which went into effect in January 1995. The accord permits the free exchange of approximately twelve thousand different products—nearly three-quarters of the goods produced in either country. The TLC established a timeline to continue introducing products until, within ten years, all goods flow back and forth in an unrestricted manner.

The treaty's signing awakened the desires of the business community to supply the sizable Mexican market with Costa Rican exports; however, there was substantial debate about the possible adverse consequences of the agreement. Several legislators expressed misgivings that the treaty was not based on any comprehensive development and trade strategy but rather was another case of Costa Rica responding to foreign pressure for economic liberalization. Mexican demand for cheap Costa Rican products, they predicted, would deplete the domestic market of its supplies. Furthermore, small and medium-sized Mexican businesses, displaced from their markets by U.S. and Canadian imports under the North American Free Trade Agreement (NAFTA), would set up shop in Costa Rica and undermine local enterprises.[17] Legislators also pointed out that the treaty made no provisions for protecting labor rights or the environment.

At an industry-specific level, the TLC raised concerns that Mexican companies would come to dominate the domestic bread industry, using flour imported from Mexico.[18] Critics also pointed out several inconsistencies in the negotiation of tariff protections. Mexican beef, for example, would enter Costa Rica free of tariffs while Costa Rican meat exporters would enjoy no such benefits.

The wealth of concerns surrounding the TLC were compounded in the waning moments of 1994 when the Mexican government announced plans to allow its peso to float on international currency markets, resulting in a near 50 percent devaluation of the currency. Free trade opponents predicted that these developments would place Mexican producers—with their technological superiority—in a position to swamp Costa Rica with lower priced and higher quality goods, while increasing the cost of Costa Rican exports to Mexico.[19] Devaluation also shrunk the size of the Mexican market as the country fell into a deep recession.

The free trade treaty with Mexico is a kind of Pandora's box that opens up myriad possibilities but with no clue as to what consequences it will bring. Although it is unclear to what extent the TLC will benefit Costa Rica, it does seem certain that it will redefine the nature of Costa Rican foreign commerce and the character of foreign investment in the country. The agreement establishes a new framework for Costa Rica's relations outside the region and its place in the global political and economic system.

Costa Rica's unilateral move to sign a trade accord with Mexico created yet another obstacle to integrationist efforts in the isthmus region. A common extraregional tariff policy is now impossible and the Central American countries fear that the agreement will convert Costa Rica into a bridge across which Mexican goods will flood, tariff-free, into their markets. The rest of Central America may be forced to follow Costa Rica's example and establish bilateral trade negotiations with Mexico simply in defense of their economic stability.

Although negotiations have proceeded at a much slower pace, free trade treaties similar to the Mexican accord are also in the works for Colombia and Venezuela. In contrast to their enthusiastic approval of the TLC, several local business groups have cautioned against similar trade agreements with South America because much of the exportable production from these countries matches Costa Rica's export offerings (including coffee, flowers, vegetables, and bananas). Trade negotiations with Venezuela and Colombia are nothing new; since 1993 the Central American republics have pursued economic ties with their southern neighbors through the proposed Investment and Commerce Accord. Extending their diplomatic reach even further, Costa Rican business and political leaders have also initiated bilateral trade talks with Chile. The southern cone country has expressed a marked interest in expanding its range of free trade into the Central American isthmus.

A member of the World Trade Organization (WTO), the successor to GATT, Costa Rica also participates in multilateral trade accords that reach beyond Latin America. It is a beneficiary of the Generalized System of Preferences (GSP) and the Caribbean Basin Initiative (CBI), which give preferential trading rights to Central American and Caribbean countries. These measures provide a strong incentive for Costa Rican exporters to send their products northward and can be identified as the source of strong growth in Costa Rican sales in the exterior in the last decade. As a part of a Central American trade bloc, some Costa Rican products also enjoy preferential treatment in the EU. This commercial agreement expired at the end of 1994, but the region managed to negotiate an extension of one year.

Although not a trade accord that involves Costa Rica directly, the North American Free Trade Agreement (NAFTA) between Mexico, the United States, and Canada has cast an entirely new and unpredictable light on the country's trade future. Despite determined lobbying efforts by Costa Rican officials, the United States has steadfastly resisted bilateral agreements aimed at including the Central American nation in the NAFTA treaty. As a result, Costa Rica has had to rejoin regional initiatives demanding that the United States grant trade protections to Central American textiles similar to those accorded to Mexican textile production. The transnationalized textile industry is a leading source of employment in the region; there is widespread fear that NAFTA could undermine the comparative advantage that Central America has enjoyed because of its low-cost labor and special trade privileges with the United States, causing companies to pick up and go to Mexico.

Central America's efforts to gain membership in NAFTA have met with little success. Nevertheless, during the 1994 Summit of the Americas regional leaders set into motion plans to establish a continental free trade zone connecting the countries of the hemisphere by the year 2005. Hemispheric free trade would undoubtedly have enormous impact on Costa Rica's other free trade negotiations in Latin America and abroad.

Although the political discourse surrounding globalization typically focuses on issues of free trade, economic integration has had other important implications for Costa Rica. Most of the country's agreements with the United States, for example, have stipulations concerning labor policy, human rights, the environment, and democratization, and thus have strongly influenced internal policymaking. Clear examples of such qualified free trade are found in the GSP and CBI, which grant preferential trade treatment on the condition that Costa Rica obeys a host of provisions regarding U.S. expropriations, satellite signal reception, intellectual property, the treatment of U.S. investors, and labor organizing.

In 1993 the AFL-CIO, the main U.S. labor federation, filed suit against Costa Rica in a U.S. court for the country's failure to abide by labor codes set forth in international accords. Threatened with suspension of the country's preferential trade status, the government rapidly approved labor laws that for several years had been mired in the legislative process. The incident was an excellent example not only of the conditionality of free trade agreements but also of globalizing trends in law and labor rights.

Both the failure to compensate U.S. citizens for property expropriations and the banana export agreements with the EU are issues threatening Costa Rica's trade negotiations with the United States. The security of preferential trade was similarly thrown into question when the Costa Rican government (for constitutional reasons) prohibited the U.S. business MILICOM from establishing a country-wide cellular telephone system.

Economic globalization is redefining not only the movement of goods and capital across national boundaries but also the meaning of political autonomy for Costa Rica and other, similarly small, underdeveloped countries. Where does sovereignty begin and end in a world where economic borders are suddenly dissolving? Depending on the interests involved, this loss of control of national economies can either be seen as an intervention in domestic affairs and a loss of national sovereignty or as an inevitable consequence of global economic integration.

Part 7

Foreign Influence

© Steven Rubin/Impact Visuals

U.S. Foreign Policy

Costa Rica, a longtime ally of the United States, received special attention from Washington during the 1980s as a result of U.S. preoccupation with Nicaragua. In marked contrast to its destabilization campaign against the Sandinista government, Washington launched an expensive stabilization effort in Costa Rica, which was promoted as a showcase of capitalist and democratic development. Tensions arose in the mid-1980s when Costa Rica began to resist U.S. attempts to involve it further in the contra war. The independence shown by President Arias in helping set the regional peace accords in motion was also a cause of tension in U.S.-Costa Rican relations. While generally a firm ally, Costa Rica also has displayed a liberal streak that Washington has not appreciated.

In 1955 U.S. Ambassador Robert Woodward reported to the State Department that Costa Rica's security forces "are handicapped in arresting communists because of the protection afforded the individual in the Costa Rican Constitution." But he noted that the "application of limited force" was possible if the United States provided Costa Rica with adequate intelligence and helped convince the public that "communism constituted a present menace." Furthermore, Woodward suggested that the public be "conditioned" to "the use of force by the authorities" by means of "a strong propaganda campaign."[1]

Through the years, U.S. government officials in Costa Rica criticized aspects of Costa Rican government as being "socialistic." Costa Rica's early support for the Sandinistas, and the principled defense of revolutionary Nicaragua offered by José Figueres Ferrer also irked Washington, as did the independence shown by President Arias in the regional peace process.

While the Costa Rican government has often shown more independence than Washington would like, it has proved a reliable U.S. ally in the region on many occasions. President José Figueres Ferrer, for example, opened the door to American Institute for Free Labor

Development (AIFLD) labor operations within the country and backed the Bay of Pigs invasion of Cuba. Receiving some funding, Figueres even collaborated with moderates within the CIA, but by the mid-1960s began expressing serious reservations about U.S. foreign policy in Latin America.

Although Costa Rica has always provided a friendly climate for U.S. investment and settlement, it was not until after 1982 that it began receiving substantial monetary rewards from Uncle Sam. These financial benefits accrued in return for Costa Rica's cooperation with the U.S. anti-Sandinista campaign. Costa Rica reluctantly allowed its territory to be used to mount the contras' southern front, and the country's media became a mouthpiece for U.S. anti-Sandinista propaganda. In violation of its own stated commitment to peace and neutrality, sectors of the Costa Rican government also permitted the United States to bolster the capabilities of the country's police forces.

The foreign policy of the Reagan administration and the peace initiatives of President Arias represented tactical differences in their attempts to modify the Nicaraguan revolution. While Reagan was still holding firm to the military option, Arias, with support from congressional Democrats and other U.S. foreign policy tacticians, recognized the futility of the contra war and advocated a negotiated settlement based on the full democratization of Nicaragua.

The Arias peace initiatives did help to undermine the contras and abate the war. But the Nicaraguan government and other observers of the peace process came to question the sincerity of Arias' commitment to regional peace and democracy given his practice of singling out Nicaragua as the main violator of the accords. While disparities in strategy continued to exist between the foreign policy approaches of the U.S. and the Costa Rican governments, President Arias consistently echoed the rhetoric in Washington about Nicaragua being the main threat to democracy in the region. He repeatedly referred to the military-controlled governments of Honduras, Guatemala, and El Salvador as democracies while labeling Nicaragua a marxist dictatorship. Following President Arias' trip to Washington in April 1989, the White House called Arias a very valuable ally to whom the administration looked for leadership "as we try to apply diplomatic pressure to Nicaragua to live up to its promises."

Washington's foreign policy in regard to Costa Rica cannot be separated from its efforts to destabilize Nicaragua. While this anti-Sandinista policy caused some inconveniences for Costa Rica, such as societal disruption and deceptions associated with the contra presence, it also proved to be the salvation of an economy on the edge of bankruptcy. The less-than-compliant position of Arias did lead to cutbacks and delays in U.S. aid designed to express U.S. displeasure.

But AID noted in its 1989 congressional presentation: "Costa Rica will continue to require significant economic assistance over the next few years to avoid deterioration of living standards....The social and political risks of such a decline are contrary to U.S. interests in the region."[2]

Costa Ricans continue to be receptive to U.S. influence, especially when it means dollars flowing into the economy. But accelerated U.S. intervention in the country's internal affairs, such as the shaping of Costa Rica's economic and foreign policies, grated on the sensibilities of many Costa Ricans. A symbol of the deepening U.S. presence and influence is one that few have missed: the construction of an imposing, new fortress-like embassy that cost $11 million and houses 225 employees. Blocks away is an equally commanding new structure that contains the AID complex of offices. Some find this concrete demonstration of U.S. commitment to the country reassuring while others see the buildings to be self-indulgent manifestations of U.S. imperial might.

By the late 1980s U.S. foreign policy attention was shifting away from Central America. Although Washington's geopolitical concerns in the region diminished, it continued to push forward its agenda of conservative economic reform and free trade in the early 1990s. It expressed its pleasure with new austerity measures that reduced the public sector's payroll and with the President Calderón's commitment to promote private sector interests, particularly those of U.S. traders and investors.

U.S.-Costa Rican relations during the Calderón government dwindled until little remained but negotiations surrounding commercial trade. Mutual disinterest played a key role in the distancing between the two countries. Costa Rica realized the unlikelihood of continued U.S. financial aid. And after the overthrow of Panama in 1989, compounded by the descent of the Sandinistas in 1990, the United States was far less concerned about maintaining a strong security presence in the region. The two year absence of a U.S. ambassador in San José was a telling sign that the United States had all but lost interest in its Central American ally. Strangely enough, the one major diplomatic issue that did emerge between 1990 and 1994, the controversy over the secretary general position of the OAS, pitted the Calderón administration against the United States. The conflict was doubly ironic given that the U.S. Republican Party supported Calderón throughout his electoral campaign.

With the regional political situation relatively stabilized and foreign policy discussions bounded by the issue of free trade, the government of José María Figueres has pursued U.S. support for a new initiative in Central America—that of sustainable development. It seems unlikely, however, that Washington will have eyes for anything but the defense of its economic interests and perhaps concerns over U.S. security (drugs, migration, infectious diseases). As the century draws to a close, bilateral dialogue between Costa Rica and the United States will probably stick to the issue of future commercial relations. Accordingly in May of 1994 Vice-President Al Gore met with the Central American presidents to announce the creation of an "Interim Trade Program" for the CBI.

U.S. Trade and Investment

To the first-time visitor, the extent of U.S. influence in Costa Rica is startling. Menus in the classier restaurants are commonly bilingual, U.S. brand-name products are readily available, and there is a large U.S. community. Sale signs for choice houses and property are frequently only in English. To an extent not seen elsewhere in Central America, Costa Rica has been inundated with American consumer culture—in the food people eat, the style of dress they wear, and even the brand of political ideology they endorse. To a large degree, the dominance of U.S. trade and investment is responsible for this saturation of consumer culture. But there is also an active identification on the part of Costa Rican society with anything and everything made in the USA.

Trade with the United States dwarfs commercial relations with other countries. About 48 percent of the country's exports (mostly coffee, bananas, and beef) are sold to the United States and 43 percent of its imports (chemicals, industrial raw materials, consumer goods, vehicles, machinery, and grains) come from the United States.[3]

Some 300 U.S. firms do business in Costa Rica, accounting for $385 million worth of investment.[4] Over one-third of these transnational corporations (TNCs) are in the manufacturing sector. The top U.S. pharmaceutical corporations have operations in Costa Rica. Many TNCs take advantage of the country's cheap labor to assemble products as diverse as nuclear gauges, golf carts, yachts, and bird cages. A small town southeast of San José supplies the U.S. Major Leagues with their yearly contingent of baseballs. Movie Star Inc., produces underpants for export, Lovable manufactures a full line of women's lingerie, and Consolidated Foods assembles bras. Costa Rica also has several clothing manufacturers that subcontract assembly work with large U.S. clothing companies. Over 20 TNCs either manufacture or distribute chemicals (mostly pesticides and fertilizers). Several of the top 20 TNC food processors produce for the nation's internal market. Colgate-Palmolive markets toothpaste and also manufactures candy, chocolates, and crackers through its subsidiary, Pozuelo.

An impressive array of business equipment corporations, including IBM, Honeywell, ITT, and Xerox, market their products within the country. Most of the top U.S. accounting firms have offices in Costa Rica, primarily to tend to the books of the other TNCs; and the top two U.S. banks—Citicorp and BankAmerica—serve the TNCs active in the country. Also in the service sector are McDonald's, KFC, Burger King, Taco Bell and Pizza Hut.

All three banana companies—Castle & Cooke, United Brands, and RJ Reynolds—have agribusiness operations, although United Brands pulled out of its banana investments in 1984 while retaining its palm oil investment. IU International has interests in sugar production, while Hershey and IC Industries are involved in the cocoa industry. Eight U.S. companies, including American Flower and Foliage, Inc., dominate the ornamental flower and plant business.

On several occasions, the U.S. embassy has used its economic aid package as leverage to ensure better treatment of U.S. investors. One case in the late 1980s involved a U.S. contractor named Jack Parker, who was suing the Costa Rican government for a breach of contract. Senator Jesse Helms took up his case and eventually the U.S. embassy threatened to freeze aid if the case was not settled favorably. Reacting to this interference, the government's Public Works minister charged that Costa Rica was being treated like a banana republic.

Tico business interests express deepening resentment at their government's favored treatment of U.S. investors. Special incentives—including tax credit certificates and exemptions from import and export duties—available to U.S. investors are often not offered to local investors.

Another group selected for special treatment is the large community of foreign settlers who qualify for pensioner status in Costa Rica. To qualify for this special status (or an associated one called *rentista*) a foreigner has to receive $600 to $1,000 monthly from sources outside the country. This person then has the right to import (duty-free) a car, electronic items, and other household goods that are prohibitively expensive for Costa Ricans due to steep import taxes. The country's relatively advanced economic state and the government's efforts to attract foreigners have resulted in an extensive expatriate community in Costa Rica. Some 7,000 heads of households have been granted the special resident status, although many more foreigners live in Costa Rica as tourists, leaving the country every 90 days to renew their visas. The pensioners have their own association, which has successfully fought off recent government attempts to chip away at their benefits in an effort to create more government revenue. About one-third of the pensioners are retired U.S. citizens; the balance are Chinese, European, and Canadian.

The 1970s and early 1980s were lean years in Costa Rica both for tourism and for foreigners seeking residency in Costa Rica. However, the international attention focused on Costa Rica as a result of Arias' Nobel Peace Prize and the government's own efforts to promote itself as an "escape to paradise" opened the doors to a new stream of foreigners seeking a peaceful tropical nirvana.

Foreigners are not only enjoying the beauty of Costa Rica, they are also buying and fencing it. In many areas, land prices have soared as foreigners have purchased choice sections of real estate. The English-language *Tico Times* runs several pages of ads for beachfront estates, plantations, and mountain hideaways. The American Realty Company entices the prospective buyer to "own your own plantation" or acquire over 2,000 acres of "rolling farmland for cattle and citrus." According to Terry Ennis, a realtor and director of the Pensioners Association, over 60 percent of Pacific Coast beachfront property is in the hands of foreigners.[5] The real estate market has been dollarized to an extraordinary level precipitating growing levels of property speculation. In 1986 an apartment 80 square meters in size in an exclusive neighborhood of San José cost little more than $25,000—its value now easily surpasses $60,000. On any given day the newspapers advertise dozens of properties (of no more than 300 sq m) whose prices surpass $200,000.

Because land speculation is common among foreign buyers, U.S. landowners have become the target of *precaristas*, the landless campesinos who squat on uncultivated land. In several cases, the *precaristas* asserted that these foreign owners were using their land as transshipment points for drugs and were themselves involved in drug trafficking. One large landowner thus implicated was John Hull, a CIA functionary who helped organize the contras' southern front.

U.S. Economic Aid

Spread across a block of land on the outskirts of San José, the mammoth Agency for International Development (AID) headquarters is surrounded by the luxury homes of the country's *nouveau riche*. One *Tico Times* reporter described the complex as "a monument to what some Costa Ricans are calling the parallel state." The $10 million building, christened "an appropriate capitol building for the parallel state," was the center for the U.S. government's efforts to stabilize and privatize the Costa Rican economy during most of the 1980s.[6] Like the nearby embassy, the AID headquarters is designed as a fortress with a rooftop heliport, emergency exits, and steel-reinforced concrete walls said to be tank-proof and unscalable.[7]

The term "parallel state" became part of the common political vocabulary in 1988 when a close adviser to President Arias, economist John Biehl, charged that AID was creating an infrastructure of private sector institutions designed to undermine corresponding public ministries and agencies. The media and business elite were indignant, and the adviser was quickly removed from government. But the term "parallel state" stuck, and for many Costa Ricans remains the most apt description of AID operations.

The U.S. economic assistance program to Costa Rica began in 1946, but it was not until the early 1980s that the country became a major recipient. In 1978 President Carter was considering removing Costa Rica from the list of AID beneficiaries because of the country's relatively high per capita income.[8] Instead, the level of aid was dramatically increased beginning in the early 1980s. From 1983-90 Costa Rica received over $1.1 billion from AID.

The floodgates of economic assistance opened because of Costa Rica's newly acquired strategic importance as the southern neighbor of revolutionary Nicaragua. Costa Rica's rising political star coincided with its rapidly deteriorating economic fortunes. Just as Washington was developing a policy of containment and counterrevolution for

Central America, Costa Rica was showing signs of economic collapse. In 1981 the country had stopped payment on its foreign debt because the national treasury was empty.

The focus of U.S. aid has been economic stabilization. Very little of the funds pumped into the country have been from AID's Development Assistance budget. Instead, virtually all the aid has come in the form of balance-of-payments support (either through the Economic Support Fund, ESF, or the PL480 Title I food-aid program), designed to improve the country's foreign exchange reserves while giving the government a flexible source of local revenue.[9] In addition to a small amount of Development Assistance, the U.S. economic-aid package includes a Peace Corps presence, a large scholarship program, and various credit and insurance arrangements sponsored by the U.S. Departments of Commerce, Agriculture, and Treasury.

Balance-of-payments support was the main thrust of AID's economic stabilization plan for Costa Rica. An entire other level of U.S. strategy comes into play, however, with the use of the local currency created by all the U.S. dollars and food pumped into the domestic economy. For the most part, AID has directed these funds into two interrelated strategies of economic development: private sector support

Figure 7a

U.S. Economic Aid to Costa Rica

In millions of U.S. $

Year	DA	ESF	PL480 Tit. I	PL480 Tit. II	Peace Corps	Total
1983	27.2	157.0	28.0	0.9	1.7	214.1
1984	15.5	130.0	22.5	—	1.8	169.8
1985	25.9	169.6	21.4	0.2	2.9	220.0
1986	13.2	126.0	20.0	0.3	2.6	162.1
1987	18.3	142.5	17.2	0.1	3.0	181.1
1988	11.3	90.0	15.0	0.1	3.5	119.9
1989	21.3	93.5	—	3.4	3.5	121.7
1990	12.6	64.9	15.0	0.2	2.2	94.9
1991	15.1	27.0	—	—	2.1	44.2
1992	12.5	11.9	—	0.1	1.9	26.4
1993	7.9	1.5	15.0	0.3	2.3	27.0
1994	3.3	—	—	1.0	2.1	6.4

DA = Development Assistance

ESF = Economic Support Funds

PL480 = Food for Peace Program.

SOURCES: U.S. Overseas Loans and Grants and Assistance from International Ogranizations 1983, 1987, 1990, 1993.

and the promotion of nontraditional exports. It is mainly here, in the allocation of these local currency funds, where the so-called "parallel state" has emerged (Figure 7a).

Assisting the Private Sector

Although private sector support has long been an element in AID's development philosophy, the Reagan administration converted it into the common denominator of the agency's development programs. In Costa Rica, this thrust took two directions: 1) a drive to privatize many public corporations and agencies, and 2) a multifaceted plan to bolster the country's business elite. Both phases of this private support strategy have received vigorous support by the country's major media, the business community itself, and leading elements within the country's two major political parties. AID monies have financed a public relations campaign that promotes the politics of private sector support. The ubiquitous slogan of this campaign, which parallels similar campaigns throughout the region, equates democracy with unrestricted capitalism.

The privatization strategy garnered widespread public sympathy for its targeting of the bureaucratic inefficiency and corruption prevalent in many government institutions. One target, CODESA, was a white elephant of a development corporation that just about everybody agrees should die. But privatization tentacles have also made gestures toward the electric and telephone companies, the state petroleum refinery, and have even threatened to engulf the National Production Council (CNP), the institution responsible for protecting the interests of grain producers and low-income consumers. Asked why AID has not demanded that all government corporations be fully privatized, Neil Billig, the director of the agency's Private Sector Office confided, "We're already twisting the government's arm as hard as we can....We can't do it all, some are sacred cows."[10] AID's Private Sector Office has recognized that it must tread carefully in its privatization drive. It has adopted what it calls a "less inflammatory" and "low profile approach to further privatization."[11]

Closely associated with the privatization drive is an AID-backed plan to promote private banking in Costa Rica. According to AID, the government's banking structure is inefficient and tainted by politics. Furthermore, its control of most of the country's financial resources violates the principles of free enterprise. As a condition for continued economic assistance, in 1984 AID obligated the Costa Rican government to: 1) allow private banks to benefit from international lines of credit from foreign donors like AID, and 2) permit those banks to accept individual deposits—both previously prohibited under the country's system of nationalized banking.

The result was a proliferation of private financial institutions, a surplus of credit at these banks, and a substantial tightening of credit available to poor and working people through the government's financial system. As Ottón Solís, the country's former Planning Minister (who resigned as a result of AID's success in undermining the country's nationalized banking system) chided, "One of the corollaries of democracy is the avoidance of the concentration of wealth, which is what the national banking system has helped this country to do. It is, in fact, a fundamental mode of being in this society." [12]

Ironically, AID's rush to support private banking with economic aid funds resulted in a highly dependent and subsidized sector. Over 40 percent of the assets held by private banks came from AID credit lines. [13] Thus, like the public sector institutions with which it is now competing, private finance was underwritten with public funds. AID acknowledged that the credit lines it offered the banks actually permitted them to provide subsidized loans to the business community.

According to Solís, this subsidized support for private banking contradicts the private enterprise and free market standards proclaimed by AID and the advocates of conservative economic policies. At the same time credit for small farmers and individual consumers can only be obtained at prohibitively high market rates (often over 30 percent). Because of the zeal shown by AID and other foreign donors in supporting private finance in Costa Rica, the banks are flooded with cheap money for which they cannot find enough outlets. The local private sector is still not ready to risk the quantity of new investment needed to pull the economy out of its slump—despite the ready supply of subsidized credit.

The other parts of AID's private sector support effort have included both the shoring up of business associations and the offering of incentives and subsidies to private investment. It is AID's contention that private sector institutions need to take a more prominent role both in the formation of national economic policy and in the promotion of investment in Costa Rica. Given the lack of a preexisting Costa Rican business organization capable of assuming this role, AID created the Coalition of Initiatives for Development (CINDE), which AID has infused with tens of millions of dollars since 1983.

To critics of AID, CINDE represents the paramount example of the "parallel state." Rather than channeling agricultural assistance, investment promotion, credit, and industrial development funds through government institutions, AID chose to hatch a new organization to receive its grants. The government has an export promotion agency, the Center for the Promotion of Exports and Investments

(CENPRO), whose effectiveness has been limited by a small budget and low salaries. Rather than working with CENPRO, AID devised a component of CINDE, known as the Investment Promotion Program (PIE), to undertake the same functions. The difference is that PIE has a multimillion dollar budget and can attract the best talent with salary levels comparable to the United States. PIE, for example, spends $1 million annually simply to operate four foreign promotional offices (three in the United States and one in Paris).

Other instances of this "parallel state" include the Private Agricultural and Agroindustrial Council (CAAP), which, like PIE, budded as a branch of CINDE. The activities of CAAP parallel those of the Ministry of Agriculture, but are exclusively oriented to the promotion of agroexport production. A revealing display of teamwork was exhibited when CAAP rallied the private sector lobby to push through the Legislative Assembly's authorization of the controversial EARTH (Agricultural School for the Humid Tropics), yet another AID-created parallel institution designed to serve only 400 students.

AID's plan to spend $118 million to establish EARTH sparked vociferous opposition among the academic community. Students, professors, and a university rector joined in the protest, arguing that the school was not necessary and contributed to the undermining of the government's higher education system. While the government's own budget was being squeezed by economic policies fostered by AID, the U.S. government was spending over a hundred million dollars to build a school that most Costa Ricans thought unnecessary. Resentment toward EARTH also represented a more general concern about the rise of private schools and universities, some of which also received AID funds.

In addition, AID has given birth to an array of research, educational, and community development organizations that together form part of an AID-controlled private infrastructure.[14] One such institution is the Center for Political-Administration Training (CIAPA), a rightwing think tank that was a center for attacks on the regional peace plan. This ideological support network provides a powerful base for the neoliberal and export-oriented strategies promoted by AID, while undermining the social structure established by the reformist state in Costa Rica.

Addressing the issue of the "parallel state," John Biehl observed, "They ended up with this fiction: When something is financed with Costa Rican taxpayers' money, it's public sector and inefficient. When the same thing is financed by U.S. taxpayers' money, it's private sector and efficient."

In 1987 an AID Inspector General report highlighted the corrupt and often ineffective nature of AID-financed programs in Costa Rica.

The report lambasted CINDE both for lacking the managerial capacity to administer the large AID grants and for its inability to produce tangible results as AID money for privatization was siphoned off through loans to the directors of CINDE and other AID projects. According to the audit report, "This organization [CINDE] has done little to promote development, but appears to have been utilized by a few prominent Costa Ricans to advance their own personal and political interests, and as a temporary resting place or springboard for aspiring politicians." Even the Central America Peace Scholarship (CAPS) program administered by AID was abused, with the sons, daughters, and relatives of some of the country's most influential families receiving scholarships targeted for the poor.[15]

Beginning in 1987 CINDE's two principal programs, PIE and the CAAP, began to show some results. The country's macroeconomic indicators were improving and U.S. investments in employment generation were on the rise. In 1987 the amount of investment required to generate an employee position reached $465, much less than the $824 estimated for the 1986-90 period and less still than AID's experiences in most other underdeveloped countries. To generate an employee requires an investment of $3,500 in the Western Caribbean, $3,000 in Honduras, $4,250 in Thailand, and $700 in Indonesia.[16]

In 1988 the U.S. embassy faced opposition to the large injection of U.S. economic aid into the country from an unlikely source. Over half the 170 Peace Corps volunteers based in the country signed a petition objecting to the planned increase of the Peace Corps contingent to 225 volunteers.[17] Those signing the petition complained that there was already a surplus of Peace Corps staff in the country and that many communities felt they were being inundated by volunteers who, in some cases, displaced Costa Rican government workers. The petition said: "It strikes us as strange that this decision to increase volunteer placement in Central America was not based on requests by community groups or Peace Corps program managers, but rather was originated and decided upon in Washington. This points to political considerations behind the decision."[18]

The results are not yet in on the full success or failure of AID's intervention in Costa Rica. AID can point to a tripling of nontraditional exports, but the development impact of this achievement is undercut by various factors: 1) a good part of the investment in nontraditional export production is in the hands of U.S. investors who repatriate their profits; 2) nontraditional exports from the industrial sector are almost entirely assembly-type manufactured goods, which provide little direct investment or value-added components to the Costa Rican economy; 3) the low aggregate value of manufactured products combined with a massive increase in imports have upset the nation's trade balance; 4) the manufacturing sector shares little vertical integration with national industries that could provide inputs and raw materials; and 5) the success of nontraditional exports can largely be attributed to government financial incentives, which have boosted the fiscal deficit.

Although the injection of large sums of U.S. economic aid have indeed allowed Costa Rica to escape the clutches of financial bankruptcy, there is much uncertainty about whether the structural adjustments imposed by AID and other international institutions have equipped the country with the economic base and direction it needs for long-term stability.

The End of Help

Since the mid-1980s the level of aid received by Costa Rica has been declining. In 1985, Luis Monge's last year in office, the country received over $220 million. By the late 1980s the country could only count on $120 million in U.S. aid. Economic aid was down to $95 million in 1990 and $27 million for 1993. For 1994 and 1995, however, economic help will hover around $6 million dollars and will probably stay near that level for the rest of the decade. AID predicts that it will close its San José office on September 30, 1996.[19] Ironically, after years of working to strengthen the political and economic capacities of a select circle of prominent businesspeople, the fortress where the AID offices are situated will probably become the new president's quarters.

Politics and economics have both figured into this pattern of decreasing U.S. aid. On the political side, the need to reward Costa Rica with *quid pro quo* aid decreased as the U.S. military campaign against Nicaragua was scaled down. Washington also found that it was not getting the *quid* for its *quo* from the Arias government. By calling off the special deals that allowed the United States to use Costa Rica as the "southern front," President Arias was punished with decreasing commitments of U.S. aid. Republican wrath with Arias was balanced, at least in part, by warm relations with the Democrats in Congress. But this alliance with the Democrats supporting the regional peace plan did not pay off in the economic dividends expected by Arias. Neither did his political initiatives pay off in terms of increased European aid.

The political tension between the Arias government and the White House certainly was a factor in aid cutbacks in the late 1980s. But AID never promised Costa Rica a future bankrolled by economic aid. After more than a billion dollars in direct economic aid in addition to an infusion of multilateral assistance, the Costa Rican economy has emerged from its earlier crisis. In AID's terms, it has been stabilized, making it harder to justify the authorization of further large sums of ESF money.

By 1990 it also became more difficult to justify large Development Assistance grants to this middle-income country, especially when the U.S. foreign aid budget was falling. The installation of a new government in Panama in December 1989 and the Sandinistas' electoral defeat two months later also meant that the strategic importance of Costa Rica had diminished. Yet the dramatic drop in economic aid has not discouraged AID from using its aid package as leverage for conservative policy reforms. The agency said it would use its future aid to support policy dialogue in four strategic areas: economic growth with improved competitiveness, democracy, more streamlined and efficient government, and environmental maintenance, mainly of natural forest habitat.[20]

U.S. Military Aid

After a lapse of 14 years Washington began supplying military aid and police training to Costa Rica in 1981. At that time, former Ambassador to the United Nations Jeane Kirkpatrick insisted that Costa Rica accept "security assistance" as a condition for increased economic aid. Both U.S. and Costa Rican officials have denied that U.S. military aid undermines the country's professed commitment to neutrality and demilitarization. Through the International Military Education and Training (IMET) and Military Assistance Program (MAP), over $32.9 million had been donated to the country in military assistance between 1980 and 1993. For fiscal year 1995 the United States allocated $50 thousand for the IMET program to be utilized in "counternarcotics operations training, pilot training, search and rescue, medical, and various other types of technical courses."[21] Costa Rican forces have received helicopters, jeeps, mortars, munitions, and a wide selection of high-powered rifles. Over 1200 members of Costa Rica's security forces have been trained locally by U.S. Mobile Training Teams (MTT) in addition to some 300 trained outside the country in Panama and at Fort Benning, Georgia.

During the 1980s and in small measure after 1990, civic action projects by U.S. National Guard and Army units have become an annual event in Costa Rica. In 1989 some 750 U.S. soldiers arrived to build bridges and roads in the isolated Osa Peninsula as part of a program that the U.S. embassy dubbed "Roads for Peace." Besides road and bridge construction, U.S. military/civic action programs have also drilled wells, repaired school buildings, and provided medical assistance. The programs have the dual purpose of generating goodwill towards the U.S. military and of providing military engineer and medical units with valuable experience in tropical areas.

With the sometimes halting cooperation of the Costa Rica government, Washington supported the southern front of the contra war along the country's northern border with Nicaragua. The corruption, intrigue, and depravity associated with that operation continues to plague U.S.-Costa Rican relations. A report on the 1984 La Penca bombing issued in late 1989 by the country's judicial authorities revealed the dirty underside of U.S. foreign policy operations in the 1980s. The report placed blame for the bombing, which occurred at a contra camp in Nicaragua just across the Costa Rican border, on contra supporters in the U.S., the CIA, and the FDN, which was the dominant contra group. Although targeting maverick contra leader Edén Pastora, the bombing killed three journalists attending a news conference and injured a dozen more, including Tony Avirgan. The report confirmed claims by Avirgan and Martha Honey that the CIA had formed a unit called the "Babies" within Costa Rica's Intelligence and Security Department (DIS) that took orders directly from the CIA. It also recommended that U.S. rancher/CIA operative John Hull and CIA operative Felipe Vidal be charged with first-degree murder for the bombing.[22]

Other Foreign Interests

Although the United States dominates trade, investment, and foreign aid programs, Costa Rica also maintains close ties with Taiwan, West Germany, and Israel. In the period 1975-85 trade with the European Union (EU) remained stable. Between 1988 and 1992 exports to the EU, mostly bananas, grew modestly from 25 to 27 percent of all Costa Rican exports. At the same time imports from the EU fell from 13 to 10 percent. Paralleling U.S. programs, EU economic aid to Costa Rica increased sharply in the 1980s but still was insignificant when compared with U.S. aid. While most U.S. aid comes in the form of balance-of-payments support, virtually all of the $40 million in EU assistance was in the form of technical assistance and credit.

West Germany is Costa Rica's main EU trading partner. The West German group most active in Costa Rica is the Ebert Foundation, which finances the PLN's training courses for community, cooperative, and political leaders. The conservative Konrad Adenauer Foundation finances the John XXIII Social School.

In recent years Costa Rica has tightened diplomatic relations with Mexico, culminating in the signing of the Free Trade Treaty, which took effect in 1995. The country currently experiences an unprecedented expansion of Mexican investments in areas ranging from tourism to food processing.

The Figueres government hopes to boost its leadership role in Central America based on initiatives to promote environmental preservation and sustainable development. Given the international reputation of its parks system, Costa Rica is in a good position to spearhead these causes.

Since the dismantling of the Berlin wall, Costa Rica has also pursued diplomatic and trade relations with former socialist bloc nations. Given the close ties that the country shares with the government of Taiwan, it is unlikely that Costa Rica will seek diplomatic relations with Beijing. Beginning in 1995, the Figueres government planned to restore diplomatic and trade relations with Cuba.

Reference Notes

Introduction

1. Samuel Z. Stone, *La Dinastía de los Conquistadores: La Crisis del Poder en la Costa Rica Contemporánea* (San José: Editorial Universitaria, 1975).
2. J.D. Trejos and M.L. Elisalde, "Costa Rica: La Distribución del Ingreso y el Acceso a los Programas de Carácter Social," (San José: Instituto de Investigaciones Económicas, Universidad de Costa Rica, 1985), p. 42.
3. Leonardo Garnier, "Crisis, Desarrollo, y Democracia en Costa Rica," *Costa Rica: Crisis y Desafíos* (San José: Departamento Ecuménico de Investigaciones/Centro de Estudios para la Acción Social-CEPAS, 1987), p. 41.

Part 1: Government and Politics

1. See Garnier, op. cit.; Manuel Rojas Bolaños, "Ocho Tesis sobre la Realidad Nacional," in *Costa Rica: Crisis y Desafíos*, op. cit.; Diego Palma, "El Estado y la Desmovilización en Costa Rica," *Estudios Sociales Centroamericanos*, No.27, 1980.
2. Excerpts of the Diego Palma essay are included in *The Costa Rica Reader*, Marc Edelman and Joanne Kenen, eds. (New York: Grove Weidenfield, 1989).
3. *Central America Report*, December 2, 1994, p. 8.
4. Jorge Rovira Más, "Costa Rica 1994: ¿Hacia la Consolidación del Bipartidismo?," *Revista Espacios*, July-September 1994.
5. *Central America Report*, February 3, 1995, p. 4.
6. Daniel García, "Costa Rica: La Subsidaria Política Exterior," *Pensamiento Propio*, March 1990.
7. *Costa Rica: Balance de la Situación*, January-March 1990.

Part 2: Economy

1. *Latin American Weekly Report*, March 15, 1990.

2. *Central America Report*, January 20, 1995, p. 4.

3. Charles D. Ameringer, *Democracy in Costa Rica* (New York: Praeger, 1982), p. 94.

4. Costa Rica Ministry of Information, *Comunicación para la Democracia*, 1984.

5. This critique is found in "Privatización: Un Nuevo Reto para los Trabajadores," *Panorama Sindical* (CEPAS), November 1987; and "La Privatización de lo Público," *Costa Rica: Balance de la Situación*, August-October 1988.

6. Manuel Solís Avendaño, *Desarrollo Rural* (San José: Editorial Universidad Estatal a Distancia-EUNED, 1981), pp. 98-100.

7. Costa Rica Ministry of Planning and Economic Policy (MIDEPLAN) and United Nations Development Program (UNDP), *Costa Rica en Cifras: 1950-1992* (San José: MIDE-PLAN, 1994).

8. Sources for this section on export crops included: Wilmer Murillo, "Transnacionales Aumentan su Poder Económico en Costa Rica," *La República*, October 28, 1988; U.S. Department of Agriculture/Foreign Agricultural Service, *Costa Rica Agricultural Situation Annual 1988*.

9. Cámara de Industrias de Costa Rica.

10. Mary Alison Clark, *Transnational Alliances and Development Strategies: The Transition to Export-led Growth in Costa Rica, 1983-1990* (Madison: University of Wisconsin-Madison, 1993), p. 279.
Clark makes a very important clarification regarding her interpretation of "success": "I use the term success here only in the narrow sense that Costa Rica clearly experienced a boom in nontraditional exports and foreign investment in these industries after 1983, during which time average GDP growth rates also returned to positive levels. Whether and how nontraditional export industries benefit developing nations is controversial. Research is currently under way on the impact of these industries on wage-workers, peasants, fishermen, regional economies, and macro-economic indicators in several countries (p. 4)."

11. Centro para la Promoción de las Exportaciones y de las Inversiones (CENPRO), *Sintesis de Exportaciones 1993*, May 1994.

12. Eliana Franco and Carlos Sojo, *Gobierno, Empresarios y Políticas de Ajuste* (San José: FLACSO, 1992), p. 68.

13. Mary Alison Clark, op. cit., p. 259.

14. Five percent of companies receive 51 percent of the total value of CATs distributed by the government.
Mary Alison Clark, op. cit., p. 264.

15. Ibid.

16. Corporación de la Zona Franca de Exportación S.A., "Análisis Comparativo Anual de la Gestión de las Empresas bajo el Régimen de Zona Franca: 1992-1993."

17. CENPRO, *Síntesis de Exportaciones 1993* (San José: CENPRO, 1994).

18. Corporación Bananera Nacional S.A., *Informe Anual de Estadísticas de Exportación de Banano 1993*.

19. A group of more than 1000 banana workers who claim to have been sterilized by agrochemicals that are produced by but prohibited in the United States currently wage a battle for redemption in U.S. courts. Approximately 5,000 workers are estimated to

have been sterilized by the indiscriminate use of agricultural chemicals in the banana industry.

20. The value of exports originating in the free trade zone sector are not included in this statistic. CENPRO, op.cit.
    The principal products for export to the United States (1993) in order of importance are: bananas, pineapples and other fresh fruits, *maquila*, beef, coffee, women's apparel, cane and beet sugars, rubber packing, shellfish, jewelry, men's apparel, flowers, ornamental plants.

21. Economist Intelligence Unit, *EIU Country Report: Costa Rica*, 1995, p. 8.

22. This data was calculated from statistics that include the value of exports that originated in the Temporary Admissions Program (*Maquila*), as well as the value of exports to Panamá. It does not include free trade zone exports, the majority of which are sent to tertiary markets.
    Banco Central de Costa Rica, "Estadísticas de los sectores Industrial Manufacturero y Explotación de Minas y Canteras: Período 1982-1992." (San José: Banco Central, July 1993), diagram 15.

23. *Rumbo* No. 515, November 1, 1994.

24. *Central America Report*, September 30, 1994.

25. The Development Group for Alternative Policy (DGAP), *Structural Adjustment in Central America: The Case of Costa Rica*, June 1993, pp. 11-19.

Part 3: Social Conditions

1. Ana Sojo, "Política Social en Costa Rica: Reformas Recientes," *Cuadernos de Ciencias Sociales* No.67 (San José: FLACSO, 1993).

2. Leonardo Garnier and Roberto Hidalgo, "El Estado Necesario y la Politica de Desarrollo," *Costa Rica entre la Ilusión y la Desesperanza: Una Alternativa para el Desarrollo* (San José: Ediciones Guayacan, 1991), p. 26.

3. J.D. Trejos, "La Politica Social y la Valorizacion de los Recursos Humanos," *Costa Rica entre la Ilusión y la Desesperanza: Una Alternativa para el Desarrollo*, op. cit., pp. 78-83.

4. Ludwig Guendel, *Analisis Retrospectivo del Desarrollo Social en Costa Rica (1950-1993)* (San José: CEPAS, July 1994).

5. J.D. Trejos, op. cit.

6. Lynn M. Morgan, "Health Effects of the Costa Rican Economic Crisis," *The Costa Rica Reader*, op. cit.

7. MIDEPLAN, *Situación Demográfica y Políticas de Población en Costa Rica*, Report to the International Conference on Population and Development, Cairo, September 1994.

8. Ludwig Guendel, op. cit.

9. *Hunger 1995: Causes of Hunger* (Washington, DC: Bread for the World, 1994).

10. United Nations Development Program (UNDP), *Informe Sobre Desarrollo Humano 1993* (Spain: UNDP, 1993).

11. *The Costa Rica Reader*, op. cit.

12. Ana Sojo, op. cit.

13. U.S. Agency for International Development (AID), *Latin America and the Caribbean Selected Economic and Social Data*, May 1994.

14. DGAP, *Structural Adjustment in Central America: The Case of Costa Rica*, June 1993, p. 19.

15. *Central America Report*, "Government Plans Under Fire," December 9, 1994.

Part 4: Civil Society

1. In Costa Rica there are 452 cooperatives with a total of 326,594 members; 424 labor unions, 160,311 members; 1,475 *solidarista* associations, 143,150 members; 1,572 development associations, 166,320 members; and 65 Cantonal Agricultural Centers, 14,998 members.
   CEPAS, *El Contexto del Desarrollo de Base en Costa Rica* (San José: Centro de Estudios para la Acción Social, 1989), p. 25, 67.

2. Diego Palma, "The State and Social Co-optation in Costa Rica," in *The Costa Rica Reader*, Marc Edelman and Joanne Kenen, eds. (New York: Grove Press, 1989).

3. Lezak Shallat, "Los Agricultores Se Enfrentan al Gobierno," *Pensamiento Propio*, September 1988.

4. Manuel Rojas Bolaños, "Ocho Tesis sobre la Realidad Nacional," op. cit., p. 26.

5. CEPAS, *El Contexto del Desarrollo de Base en Costa Rica*, op. cit., p. 67.

6. In terms of volume, large cooperatives produce 43 percent of coffee and 25 percent of meat exports. About 42 percent of milk production and 80 percent of dairy products originate in this sector. Large cooperatives also produce 20 percent of sugar, 80 percent of onions, 48 percent of potatoes.
   Ibid., p. 28.

7. National Council of Cooperatives (CONACOOP), *Memoria: Resoluciones y Acuerdos del VII Congreso Cooperativo: El Movimiento Cooperativo de Frente a los Retos del Siglo XXI* (San José: CONACOOP, 1991).

8. "El Sector Urbano Común," *Costa Rica: Balance de la Situación*, November-December 1988.

9. CEPAS, *El Contexto del Desarrollo de Base en Costa Rica*, op. cit., p. 45.

10. Isabel Román, "Costa Rica: Los Campesinos También Quieren Futuro," *Alternativas Campesinas*, CRIES, eds. (Managua: Latino Editores, 1994), p. 73.

11. CEPAS, *El Contexto del Desarrollo de Base en Costa Rica*, op. cit., p. 46.

12. Isabel Román, op. cit., p. 76.

13. Ibid., pp. 74-5.

14. Ibid., pp. 82-3.

15. *Central America Report*, October 14, 1994.

16. CEPAS, *El Contexto del Desarrollo de Base en Costa Rica*, op. cit., p. 83.

17. Ibid., p. 37.

18. Ibid.

19. U.S. Department of Labor, *Foreign Labor Trends: Costa Rica 1987-1988*.

20. *Petición de los Sindicatos Norteamericanos (AFL-CIO) para la Suspensión de los Beneficios del Sistema Generalizado de Preferencias de los Estados Unidos a Costa Rica*, Serie Documentos Oficiales (San José: Movimiento Solidarista Costarricense, 1993), p. 1.

21. Ibid., pp. 1-3.

22. Ibid., pp. 1-2.

23. Costa Rica Ministry of Planning and Economic Policy (MIDEPLAN). *Perfil Actual del Solidarismo en Costa Rica*. (San José: MIDEPLAN, July 1989), p. 2.

24. Costa Rica Legislative Assembly, *Ley de Asociaciones Solidaristas (1984)* (San José: Movimiento Solidarista Costarricense, 1984).

Reference Notes

25. According to *solidarista* organizations, in 1994 there were 1,468 associations in the country with a total of 186,750 members.

26. Curtin Winsor, Jr., "The Solidarista Movement: Labor Economics for Democracy," *The Washington Quarterly*, Fall 1986.

27. CEPAS, *El Contexto del Desarrollo de Base en Costa Rica*, op. cit., p. 33.

28. Lezak Shallat, "Solidarismo Invades Last Union Stronghold," *The Tico Times*, August 7, 1987.

29. Winsor, op. cit.

30. Oscar Ramírez Lizano, President of the National Chamber of Agriculture and Animal Husbandry (CNAA), "The Position of the National Chamber of Agriculture and Animal Husbandry (CNAA) Regarding the Economic Opening," *Costa Rica: Democracia, Económica, y Desarrollo Social Hacia el Año 2000*, pp. 73-85.

31. CEPAS, *Producción Campesina y Apertura Comercial en Centroamérica: Mecanismos de Toma de Decisiones del Sector Agropecuario* (San José: CEPAS, 1993), p. 46.

32. Ibid., p. 34.

33. Two valuable articles on media manipulation in Costa Rica are: "The Continuing War: Media Manipulation in Costa Rica" by Howard Friel and Michell Joffroy in *Covert Action Information Bulletin*, Summer 1986; and "Back in Control" by Jacqueline Sharkey in *Common Cause Magazine*, September-October 1986.

34. Much of this discussion of the history and social vision of the Catholic Church is digested from: Andrés Opazo Bernales, *Costa Rica: La Iglesia Católica y el Orden Social* (San José: Departamento Ecuménico de Investigaciones, 1987).

35. Ibid.

36. *Directorio de Iglesias, Organizaciones, y Ministros del Movimiento Protestante: Costa Rica* (San José: PROLADES, 1986).

37. Ibid.

38. In keeping with its usage in Central America, the term "evangelical" is used here to refer to all non-Catholic Christians, including pentecostals, fundamentalists, and mainline Protestants.
Ibid.

39. *World Christianity: Central America and the Caribbean*, Clifton L. Holland, ed. (Monrovia, CA: MARC/World Vision International, 1981).

40. *Rumbo*, July 1989.

41. Interview with Kris Merschrod, PACT, April 1988.

42. FLACSO, *Mujeres Latinoamericanas en Cifras: Costa Rica*, Teresa Valdés and Enrique Gomáriz, coord. (Santiago: Instituto de la Mujer/FLACSO, 1993), p. 8.

43. Obviously this average does not reveal the differences between poor rural populations and wealthier, urban groups.
Ibid., pp. 66-71.

44. Emma Daly, "Child Abuse Increasing," *The Tico Times*, April 15, 1988

45. Emma Daly, "Violence Against Women Increasing in Costa Rica," *The Tico Times*, April 8, 1988.

46. FLACSO, *Mujeres Latinoamericanas en Cifras: Costa Rica*, op. cit., pp. 38-51.

47. Ibid., pp. 99-101.

48. Inter-American Institute for Agricultural Cooperation, *La Política del Sector Agropecuario Frente a la Mujer Productora de Alimentos en Centroamérica y Panamá* (San José: IICA/BID, 1993).

49. Cited in: Abigail Adams, "Sterilization in Costa Rica," *Links* (NCAHRN), Winter 1987.

50. *Central America Report*, September 1, 1989.

51. Carolyn Hall, *Costa Rica: A Geographical Interpretation in Historical Perspective* (Boulder: Westview Press, 1985), p. 45.

52. Brian Houseal, Craig MacFarland, Guillermo Archibold, and Aurelio Chiari, "Indigenous Cultures and Protected Areas in Central America," *Cultural Survival Quarterly*, Vol.9, No.1, 1985.

53. Ibid.

54. Commission for the Defense of Human Rights in Central America (CODEHUCA), *Informe Anual 1993: Situación de los Derechos Humanos en Centroamérica* (San José: CODEHUCA, 1993), p. 25.

55. William Vargas Mora, "Intereses Foraneos Contra Indígenas de Talamanca," *Aportes*, July 1988.

56. UNDP, *CIREFCA: Balance y Estrategia Futura* (San José: UNDP, May 1994), p. 2.

57. Ibid., pp. 4-5.

58. *Central America Report*, January 27, 1995.

Part 5: Environment

1. Lucio Pedroni, *Diagnóstico Forestal de Costa Rica*, a report by the Swiss Organization for Development and Cooperation, August 1992, p. 90.

2. Guillermo Monge, "La Valorización de los Recursos Naturales y la Sostenibilidad del Desarrollo," *Costa Rica entre la Ilusión y la Desesperanza: Una Alternativa para el Desarrollo*, Garnier, Leonardo, et. al. (San José: Ediciones Guayacán, 1991), p. 112.

3. Ibid., p. 122.

4. Costa Rica Ministry of Natural Resources, Energy, and Mines (MIRENEM), *Estrategia de Conservación para el Desarrollo Sostenible de Costa Rica* (San José: Servicios Litográficos, 1990), p. 64.

5. Guillermo Monge, op.cit., pp. 117-8.

6. MIRENEM, op.cit., p. 43.

7. *La República*, "Continúa Alta Tasa de Deforestación: Tala Ilegal no Tiene Freno," August 21, 1994, p. 5A.

8. Lucio Pedroni, op.cit., p. 90.

9. Fundación Neotrópica, *Desarrollo Socioeconómico y el Ambiente Natural de Costa Rica: Situación Actual y Perspectivas*, p. 85.

10. MIRENEM, *Estrategia de Conservación para el Desarrollo Sostenible de Costa Rica*, op.cit., pp. 50-7.

11. Oscar Fallas, "Los Impactos Ambientales de los Programas de Ajuste Estructural", *Costa Rica: Balance de la Situación*, May 1994. p. 27.

12. Fundación Neotrópica. op.cit., pp. 96-7.

13. Ibid., pp. 105, 116.

14. Guillermo Monge, op.cit., p. 126.

15. Bill Weinberg, *War on the Land: The Politics of Ecology and the Ecology of Politics in Central America*, unpublished manuscript.

16. *Aportes*, December 1988. ASCONA became defunct in 1989 after having simultaneously lost its volunteer basis and its AID funding.

Part 6: Central American Integration, Free Trade Treaties, and Globalization

1. Carlos Sojo, "Centroamérica: La Nueva e Inevitable Integración," *Relaciones Internacionales*, No.42 (San José: Universidad Nacional, 1993), p. 20.

2. Alvaro López Mora, *Producción Campesina y Apertura Comercial en Centroamérica: Mecanismos de Toma de Decisiones del Sector Agropecuario*, (San José: CEPAS, 1993), p. 50.

3. Ibid p. 51.

4. Carlos Sojo, *Relaciones Internacionales*, op.cit., p. 21.

5. Sectoral forums include the Central American Agriculture and Animal Husbandry Council, the Central American Monetary Council, the councils of the Ministries of Treasury, Economy, Commerce, Industry, Infrastructure, Tourism, Services, and the Social Council.

6. Alvaro López Mora, op.cit., p. 63.

7. Ibid., p. 55.

8. Jaime Delgado Rojas, "Integración Regional: La Perspectiva Política," *Costa Rica: Balance de la Situación*, May 1994.

9. Ibid.

10. The Nicaraguan Legislative Assembly recently ratified Nicaragua's incorporation into PARLACEN, but it has yet to elect the country's representatives.

11. Carlos Sojo, op.cit., p. 23.

12. This information was calculated from data that includes the value of the exports originating in the Temporary Admissions Program (*Maquila*), as well as the value of exports to Panama. They do not include the exports from the Free Trade Zones, most of which are sent to tertiary markets.
Costa Rican Central Bank, "Estadísticas de los Sectores Industriales Manufactureros y Explotación de Minas y Canteras: Período 1982-1992" (San José: Banco Central, July 1993).

13. Interview with Roberto Rojas, Ministry of Foreign Commerce, *Panorama Internacional*, No.216, February 21, 1994, p. 21.

14. Ibid., p. 20.

15. Coalition of Initiatives for Development (CINDE), "Nuestra Posición ante Algunas Críticas al Tratado de Libre Comercio entre Costa Rica y México," *La Nación*, October 22, 1994.

16. *La Nación*, October 14, 1994.

17. *La Nación*, October 15, 1994.

18. The Mexican group GRUMA bought, through its subsidiary in Costa Rica, DEMASA, a corn meal factory, and Schmidt, Camacho, Roca, and Arro Rico bakeries, all Costa Rican-owned. The Bimbo company, also Mexican, bought the Costa Rican bakery Cinta Azul. For the moment both business groups together bake about 28 percent of the sandwich bread consumed in the country.
Rumbo, No.515, November 1, 1994.

19. *Central America Report*, January 27, 1995.

Part 7: Foreign Influence

1. Noam Chomsky, *Necessary Illusions* (Boston: South End Press, 1989), pp. 264-5.
2. AID, Congressional Presentation, FY1989.
3. Economist Intelligence Unit, *EIU Country Report: Costa Rica*, 1995, p. 8.
4. "Direct Investment Positions on a Historical-Cost Basis", *Survey of Current Business*, August 1994.
5. Interview by Debra Preusch (Resource Center), March 1989.
6. Lezak Shallat, "AID and the Parallel State," *The Costa Rica Reader*, op. cit.
7. Martha Honey, "Costa Rica: U.S. Imposes Its Ideology," *Los Angeles Times*, October 30, 1988.
8. Martha Honey, "Undermining a Friend: The Impact of Reagan/Bush Policies in Costa Rica," July 1989.
9. Both the ESF and Title I programs function as balance-of-payments support, either by injecting dollars directly into the national treasury (ESF) or shipping food commodities that would have otherwise required scarce dollars to purchase (Title I). When the coveted foreign exchange (ESF) and food (Title I) are then sold to the private sector on the local market, the government obtains a sum of local currency equal to the value of the two programs.
10. Interview by author with Neil Billig, U.S. Agency for International Development/Costa Rica, Private Sector Office, March 1989.
11. AID/Costa Rica, Private Sector Office, "Three Year Strategy," January 25, 1988.
12. Interview by author with Ottón Solís, March 1989.
13. Ibid.
14. The complete list of private organizations that receive local funds derived from AID donations can be found in Carlos Sojo, *La Mano Visible del Mercado: La Asistencia de Estados Unidos al Sector Privado Costarricense en la Década de los Ochenta* (Managua: CRIES/CEPAS, 1992).
15. Abelardo Morales Gamboa, "Ricos y Famosos Se Benefician con AID," *Aportes*, March 1988.
16. Cited by Carlos Sojo, *La Mano Visible del Mercado*, op. cit., p. 57.
17. In mid-1989, there were 215 Peace Corps volunteers assigned to Costa Rica.
18. Peter Brennan, "Peace Corps Volunteers Protest Expansion," *The Tico Times*, March 29, 1988.
19. Eliana Franco and Carlos Sojo, op. cit., p. 68.
20. Interview with James Vandenhos, Central American AID office, Washington, D.C., June 9, 1994.
21. *Congressional Presentation for Security Assistance Programs FY1995.*
22. Martha Honey has produced an extraordinary account of the most relevant facts concerning the dark underbelly of U.S. policy in Costa Rica during the 1980s in an exhaustive volume titled *Hostile Acts: U.S. Policy in Costa Rica in the 1980's* (Gainesville: University Press of Florida, 1994).

Bibliography

The following periodicals are useful sources of information and analysis on Costa Rica:

Aportes, Editorial Aportes para la Educación (San José), monthly, Spanish.

Central America Report, Inforpress Centroamericana (Guatemala), biweekly, English.

Mesoamerica, Institute for Central American Studies (San José), monthly, English.

Pensamiento Propio, Coordinadora Regional de Investigaciones Económicas y Sociales (Managua), monthly, Spanish.

Semanario Universidad, Universidad de Costa Rica (San José), weekly, Spanish.

The Tico Times (San José), weekly, English.

The following books contain valuable background on a wealth of issues important to understanding Costa Rica:

Costa Rica: Crisis y Desafíos, (San José: Departamento Ecuménico de Investigaciones/Centro de Estudios para la Acción Social-CEPAS, 1987).

The Costa Rica Reader, Marc Edelman and Joanne Kenen, eds. (New York: Grove Weidenfield, 1989).

CEPAS, *Producción Campesina y Apertura Comercial en Centroamérica: Mecanismos de Toma de Decisiones del Sector Agropecuario* (San José: CEPAS, 1993).

Mary Alison Clark, *Transnational Alliances and Development Strategies: The Transition to Export-led Growth in Costa Rica, 1983-1990* (Madison: University of Wisconsin, 1993).

Eliana Franco and Carlos Sojo, *Gobierno, Empresarios y Políticas de Ajuste* (San José: FLACSO, 1992).

Ludwig Guendel, *Analisis Retrospectivo del Desarrollo Social en Costa Rica (1950-1993)* (San José: CEPAS, July 1994).

Carolyn Hall, *Costa Rica: A Geographical Interpretation in Historical Perspective* (Boulder: Westview Press, 1985).

Karen Hansen-Kuhn, *Structural Adjustment in Central America: The Case of Costa Rica* (Washington, D.C.: The Development Group for Alternative Policy, 1993).

Martha Honey, *Hostile Acts: U.S. Policy in Costa Rica in the 1980's* (Gainesville: University Press of Florida, 1994).

Andrés Opazo Bernales, *Costa Rica: La Iglesia Católica y el Orden Social* (San José: Departamento Ecuménico de Investigaciones, 1987).

Manuel Rojas Bolaños, et.al., *La Democracia Inconclusa* (San José: DEI-IIS, 1989).

Jorge Rovira Más, *Costa Rica en los Años 80* (San José: Editorial Porvenir, 1987).

Mitchell A. Seligson, *Peasants of Costa Rica and the Development of Agrarian Capitalism* (Madison: University of Wisconsin, 1980).

Carlos Sojo, *La Utopía del Estado Mínimo: Influencia de AID en Costa Rica en los Años Ochenta* (Managua: CRIES/CEPAS, 1991).

Carlos Sojo, *La Mano Visible del Mercado: La Asistencia de Estados Unidos al Sector Privado Costarricense en la Década de los Ochenta* (Managua: CRIES/CEPAS, 1992).

The following publications are useful sources for statistical data on Costa Rica:

Instituto de la Mujer, Spain Ministry of Social Issues/Facultad Latinoamericana de Ciencias Sociales (FLACSO), *Mujeres Latinoamericanas en Cifras: Costa Rica* (Santiago: FLACSO, 1993).

Inter-American Institute for Agricultural Cooperation (IICA)/FLACSO, *Centroamérica en Cifras*. San José, Costa Rica, 1991.

Costa Rica Ministry of Planning and Economic Policy (MIDEPLAN)/United Nations Development Program (UNDP), *Costa Rica en Cifras: 1950-1992* San José, Costa Rica. 1994.

Chronology

1821	Central American region declares independence from Spain.
1822	Annexation to Mexico.
1823	Independence from Mexico as United Provinces of Central America.
	U.S. pronouncement of Monroe Doctrine.
1826	Outbreak of civil war.
1830	Morazán takes Guatemala City, becomes president of United Provinces of Central America.
1835	San José declared capital.
	Conservative Carillo takes power.
1838	Central American federation breaks into five states.
	Carillo declares himself president of Costa Rica for life.
1842	Carillo ousted by Morazán, who tries to re-establish federation.
	Morazán overthrown and executed.
1844	New Costa Rican constitution promulgated.
1849	Establishment of conservative government under Mora Porras.
1859	Mora resigns; Montealegre family takes power, which it will hold for a decade.
	New constitution promulgated.
1860	Mora leads a failed invasion attempt and is executed.
1869	New constitution promulgated.
1870	Liberal government under Guardia.
1871	New liberal constitution promulgated.
	First railroad opens Atlantic Coast to banana production.
1890	Inauguration of conservative government under Rodríguez.
	Formation of the Artisans Constitutional Club.
	Formation of the Catholic Union Party by Bishop Bernardo Augusto Thiel.
1894	Rodríguez's nominee Iglesias becomes president.
1901	Formation of the Workers League.

1902	Election of liberal Esquivel.
1906	Inconclusive election; Congress chooses liberal candidate González.
	Because it has been less involved in regional conflicts, Costa Rica begins to be seen as a natural mediator and home for exiled dissidents.
1910	Election of conservative Jiménez Oreamuno.
1913	Formation of General Confederation of Workers (CGT).
1914	Inconclusive election; Congress chooses noncandidate González Flores.
1917	Tinoco seizes power in coup and abrogates constitution.
1918	U.S. President Wilson influences the governing of Costa Rica and encourages development of oil resources.
1919	Tinoco resigns; constitution of 1871 restored.
	CGT sparks formation of Socialist Center.
1921	Latin American Mission begins its evangelizing campaigns.
1923	CGT dissolves to form Reformist Party.
1924	Jiménez Oreamuno elected for second term.
	Revision of Costa Rican Penal Code to outlaw most strikes.
1928	González elected.
1931	Formation of Communist Party (PC) under Mora Valverde.
1932	Formation of National Republican Party (PRN).
	Jiménez Oreamuno elected for third term.
1934	Massive banana worker strike led by PC.
	Formation of Costa Rican Workers Confederation (CTCR).
1936	PRN candidate Cortés elected.
1940	PRN candidate Calderón Guardia elected in landslide.
	Cortés forms Democratic Party (PD).
1941	New Labor Code recognizes right to strike; broad social security program established.
	Figueres Ferrer denounces President Calderón in radio speech and is sent into exile.
1943	PC reorganized as Popular Vanguard Party (PVP).
1944	PRN-PVP coalition candidate Picado Michalski elected.
1945	Formation of the Rerum Novarum Workers Confederation of Costa Rican (CCTRN).
1947	Formation of Democratic Renovation Party (PRD) by Carazo.
1948	
Feb.	Election won by Ulate Blanco of a coalition comprised of PD, Social Democratic Party (PSD), and National Unification Party (PUN). PRN wins majority in Congress, which annuls the presidential election results.
Mar.	Civil war breaks out; 1948 "revolution."
	Figueres receives substantial U.S. support (and later admits to CIA connections).

Chronology

Apr.	Picado overthrown by forces led by Figueres.
May	Formation of Junta of Second Republic, with Figueres acting as president.
Dec.	Picado supporters stage unsuccessful invasion attempt from Nicaragua.
1949	Ulate inaugurated as president.
	New constitution promulgated that abolishes army, franchises women, and outlaws PVP.
	Formation of the Socialist Action Party (PAS).
	Catholicism declared official religion.
	Banks nationalized.
1951	Formation of National Liberation Party (PLN) by Figueres.
1953	PLN candidate Figueres elected.
	Formation of Costa Rican General Workers Confederation (CGTC).
1955	Unsuccessful invasion attempts by exiles based in Nicaragua.
1958	PUN candidate Echandí Jiménez elected.
1961	Formation of the paramilitary Free Costa Rica Movement (MCRL).
1962	PLN candidate Orlich Bolmarich elected.
	Formation of Christian Democratic Party (PDC).
	Full relations broken with Cuba.
1963	Costa Rica joins the Central American Common Market (CACM).
1966	National Unification Coalition candidate Trejos Fernández elected.
1968	Archbishop of San José abstains from signing the Medellín document.
1969	Constitution of 1949 amended.
1970	PLN candidate Figueres elected.
	Antigovernment protest over U.S. interest denounced by government as being provoked by "communist elements."
1971	Formation of Authentic Confederation of Democratic Workers (CATD) after split with Costa Rican Confederation of Democratic Workers (CCTD).
1972	Formation of Confederation of Costa Rican Workers (CTC).
1974	Use of words "marxist" and "communist" banned during pre-election period by Supreme Tribunal of Elections.
	PLN candidate Oduber Quiros elected.
1975	Government purchase of uncultivated United Brands land
	Sexist use of women's bodies in commercial advertising banned.
	Trade relations with Cuba re-established.
	PVP returned to legal status.
1976	Splits in PLN and PUN.
	Formation of Republican Calderonista Party (PRC).
1977	Restoration of consular relations with Cuba.
	Indigenous Bill establishes right of *indigenas* to land reserves.

1978	Formation of Unity coalition including PRD, PRC, PDC, and PUP (Popular Unity Party), led by Calderón Fournier.
	Opposition Union candidate Carazo Odio elected; PVP-MRP gains three seats in legislative election.
1979	Government support of the FSLN revolutionaries in Nicaragua.
	Formation of the Unitary Confederation of Workers (CUT).
1980	Formation of Costa Rican Solidarista Union (SURSUM).
1981	United States resumes military aid and police training after 14-year lapse.
May	Parliamentary commission report on government involvement in arms trafficking to the FSLN.
	Consular relations with Cuba are broken.
Sept.	Moratorium on debt payments.
1982	PLN candidate Monge Alvarez elected.
	Government asks 17 Soviet diplomats to leave country.
	Foreign Ministers of Costa Rica, El Salvador, and Honduras form Central American Democratic Community.
1983	Contadora group meets for first time to develop dialogue and negotiation in Central America; parties to peace accords include Costa Rica, El Salvador, Guatemala, Honduras, and Nicaragua.
	Division in PVP; Mora leaves to form Costa Rican People's Party (PPC).
	Unity coalition renamed Social Christian Unity Party (PUSC) under Calderón.
	Formation of National Confederation of Workers (CNT) by American Institute for Free Labor Development (AIFLD) of the AFL-CIO.
	Presence of contras on Costa Rican territory increases tension with Nicaragua.
	Foreign debt soars 40 percent to $4 billion over a seven-month period.
	Israel begins security and intelligence training for Costa Rican police forces.
1984	Costa Rica seeks increase in military aid from United States.
	United Brands sells its banana lands but retains palm oil investments.
May	PLN organizes demonstration of 30,000 people to support neutrality with slogan "No to Armaments for Costa Rica."
	Bomb explodes during press conference of contra leader Edén Pastora in La Penca with over a dozen casualties among Costa Rican and foreign journalists.
	Formation of the environmentalist PEC.
June	Monge reaffirms Costa Rica's neutrality in U.S.-Nicaraguan conflict, but U.S. opposition leads to resignation of foreign minister.
July	Ten-week strike by banana workers begins.
Aug.	Cabinet reshuffle, rightwing shift in government.

	Agreement with USIA initiates Voice of America broadcasts in northern Costa Rica.

Sept.   IMF agreement.

Nicaragua agrees to sign Contadora treaty, but Costa Rica, El Salvador, and Honduras refuse to sign.

1985   Arrival of United States military training team.

Government receives first Structural Adjustment Loan (SAL I).

1986   Formation of the Permanent Worker Council (CPT)

Feb.   PLN candidate Arias Sánchez elected.

Arrival of United States military engineers for "Operation Peace Bridge."

June   Third revised Contadora treaty presented, Costa Rica, El Salvador, and Honduras refuse to sign.

1987

Feb.   Arias takes leadership role in regional peace initiatives, meets with representatives from El Salvador, Guatemala, and Honduras in Esquipulas, Guatemala.

Aug.   Presidents of Costa Rica, El Salvador, Guatemala, Honduras, and Nicaragua sign Esquipulas II Peace Accords.

Oct.   Arias is awarded the Nobel Prize for Peace.

Nov.   Esquipulas peace accords go into effect. Costa Rica already meets most terms of compliance except for ratification of Central American Parliament.

1988   Over half of 170 Peace Corps volunteers in Costa Rica sign petition objecting to proposed increase to 225 volunteers as being unnecessary and politically motivated.

Intense debate in legislature and media about formation of Central American Parliament and Costa Rica's participation continue through 1988 and mid-1989.

Jan.   Continued Esquipulas peace talks in San José.

Mar.   Arias accuses countries of El Salvador, Guatemala, Honduras, and Nicaragua with not complying fully with Esquipulas peace accords, and criticizes presence of U.S. troops in Honduras.

Apr.   After special request brought from White House by Morris Busby, Arias approves use of Costa Rican territory to channel humanitarian aid to the contras.

Arias travels to Washington, meets with President Bush, and requests more aid.

Arias awarded Inter-American Leadership prize by Pan American Development Fund.

The five Central American vice-presidents meet in San José to discuss Central American Parliament and agree to present regional economic cooperation plan to United Nations.

Guatemala accuses Costa Rica of noncompliance with the Esquipulas peace accords because it failed to ratify treaty to create Central American Parliament.

Aug.	U.S. special envoy Morris Busby comes to Costa Rica three times in one month, twice in company of Secretary of State George Shultz.
	Peace talks postponed twice.
Oct.	Government condemns incursion of Panamanian troops into Costa Rican territory.
	Arias asks Contadora group to back Esquipulas peace accords.
Nov.	Agreements with Nicaragua for joint patrol of common border.
1989	Structural Adjustment Loan II approved (SAL II).
	Arias accuses Nicaragua of noncompliance with peace accords. Ortega sends formal letter stating Arias inappropriately assumed verification role.
Jan.	Arias meets with U.S. ambassador, requests peace talks be postponed to February.
	Former minister of Public Security accused of being collaborator in illegal activities of National Security Council and Oliver North.
	John Hull, U.S. citizen and longtime resident of Costa Rica, arrested by Office of Judicial Investigation (OIJ) for crimes against state.
	Former president Oduber admitted receiving one million *colones* for his electoral campaign from U.S. citizen linked to drug trafficking.
Feb.	Eleven U.S. congressmen request that Arias intervene in arrest and trial of Hull.
	Esquipulas peace talks held in El Salvador after four postponements.
	Costa Rica states that because of shipping rights and potential ecological effects, an interoceanic canal cannot be built through Nicaragua on San Juan River without Costa Rican participation.
	Arias reaffirms that the five Central American presidents were very explicit in their determination to dismantle contras.
Apr.	Arias sets off on eight-day tour to Washington and Ottawa, Canada, in executive jet belonging to Del Monte.
	Costa Rica says it will not keep contra members unwilling to return to Nicaragua after they disband.
	The other four Central American nations say they will go ahead with Central American Parliament without Costa Rica, whose Congress has not yet ratified plan. Andean Parliament encourages Costa Rica to ratify plan.
	Allegations that Panamanian dictator Noriega donated suitcase full of dollars to Arias' electoral campaign.
	Former President Monge denies allegations he accepted U.S. funding for "certain operations" in exchange for supporting contras in Costa Rica.
July	Reports surface of CIA-supported anti-Noriega guerrilla forces, composed largely of ex-contras, forming along Costa Rica-Panama border.

Chronology

Aug.	John Hull jumps bail and leaves for Miami.
Dec.	U.S. troops invade Panama, ousting Noriega.
1990	PUSC candidate Calderón Fournier elected president.
	World Bank suspends SAL II payments due to high inflation rates and government expenditures.
	In Antigua Summit (also known as Central American Economic Summit) country leaders sign Central American Plan for Economic Action (PAECA).
1991	Earthquake kills 62 people, causes massive damage in port city of Limón.
	Government signs new agreement with IMF; SAL II disbursements freed.
	The Central American presidents endorse Tegucigalpa Protocol, creating System of Central American Integration (SICA).
1992	President Calderón enacts executive decree conferring permanent and temporary residence to refugees and undocumented migrants.
June	European Union (EU) announces that, beginning in 1993, it will impose system of tariffs and quotas on banana imports.
July	Dozens of *indigenas* march on Legislative Assembly to demand reforms in Indigenous Law and propose Commission of Indigenous Issues.
Sept.	Rerum Novarum Workers Confederation of Costa Rica re-forms from alliance of three different unions, CCTD, National Confederation of Workers (CNT), and CATD.
1993	AFL-CIO brings suit in U.S. courts against Costa Rican government for failure to abide by international labor laws. Government institutes reforms to avoid loss of preferential trading status with United States.
	Emergence of new Democratic Force Party (PFD).
	Country leaders sign Protocol to Treaty of Central American Economic Integration.
Feb.	Costa Rica requests that GATT form panel to analyze restrictions imposed by EU on Latin American banana imports.
March	Eight thousand farmers stage protests in San José to demand greater government attention. Organized by UPANACIONAL, demonstration wins campesinos government's commitment to devote over $300 million to development of agricultural sector.
1994	
Feb.	PLN candidate José María Figueres elected to presidency.
March	United Nations Commission on Human Rights releases report on Costa Rica's fulfillment of Political and Civil Rights Pact.
May	José María Figueres takes office.
Aug.	Four OIJ officials accused of slaying drug runner Ciro Monge Mena.

	Ex-Minister of Public Security and PUSC Presidential Precandidate Luis Fishman implicated in arms scandal involving disappearance of 4,000 weapons allocated to public forces.
Sept.	Government closes Anglo Costarricense Bank.
	More than 30 campesinos wounded in confrontation with police after occupying Rincón Grande de Pavas farm.
Oct.	Regional conference resulting in Alliance for Sustainable Development.
	Structural Adjustment Program III passed in Costa Rican legislature.
	U.S. Drug Enforcement Administration (DEA) uncovers Costa Rican links to international drug and money-laundering ring.
Nov.	Figueres announces 1994-98 Development Plan, including plan to combat poverty.
	Rafael Angel Guillén Elizondo, Director of OIJ, announces retirement amid acccusations of OIJ corruption and human rights violations.
Dec.	Costa Rica participates in Summit of the Americas.
1995	
Jan.	Free Trade Agreement with Mexico goes into effect.

SOURCES: *Encyclopedia of the Third World* (1987); *Conflict in Central America* (Longman Group Ltd, 1987); *Labor Organizations in Latin America*, Gerald Greenfield and Sheldon Maran, editors (Greenwood Press, 1987); and *Costa Rica: Balance de la Situación* (CEPAS, various issues); *Central America Report*, Inforpress Centroamericana.

For More Information

Resources

Facultad Latinoamericana de Ciencias Sociales (FLACSO),
Programa Costa Rica
Apartado 11747-1000
San José, Costa Rica

Centro de Capacitación para el Desarrollo (CECADE)
Apartado 447, San Pedro Montes de Oca
San José, Costa Rica

Aportes
Apartado Postal 103-1009 Fecosa
San José, Costa Rica

Mesoamerica
Apartado Postal 300-1002
San José, Costa Rica

Departamento Ecuménico de Investigaciones (DEI)
Apartado Postal 390-2070 Sabanilla
San José, Costa Rica

Friends Peace Center
Calle 15, Avenida 6 Bis, #1336
San José, Costa Rica

Central American Association of the Relatives of the Detained-
Disappeared (ACAFADE)
Apartado 8188-1000
San José, Costa Rica

Comisión para la Defensa de los Derechos Humanos en Cen-
troamérica (CODEHUCA)
Apartado Postal 189
Paseo de los Estudiantes
San José, Costa Rica

Tours

Institute for Central American Studies
Apartado Postal 300-1002
San José, Costa Rica

Current Events Contact
Apartado Postal 170-2070 Sabanilla
San José, Costa Rica
(Business/Official tours)

Coalición de Iniciativas de Desarrollo (CINDE)
Apartado Postal 4946-1000
San José, Costa Rica

Embassy of Costa Rica
1825 Connecticut Avenue NW
Washington, DC 20009

Embassy of the United States in Costa Rica
APO Miami, FL 34020

U.S. State Department
Citizen's Emergency Center/Travel Information
Main State Building
Washington, DC 20520
(202) 647-5225

The Resource Center

The Interhemispheric Resource Center is a private, nonprofit, research and policy institute located in New Mexico. Founded in 1979, the Resource Center produces books, policy reports, and other educational materials about U.S. foreign policy, as well as sponsoring popular education projects. For more information and a catalog of publications, please write to the Resource Center, Box 4506, Albuquerque, New Mexico 87196.

Board of Directors

Tom Barry, *Resource Center*; Rosa Delia Caudillo, *Red Fronteriza de Salud y Ambiente*; John Cavanagh, *Institute for Policy Studies*; Noam Chomsky, *Massachusetts Institute of Technology*; Mayee Crispin, *Service Employees International Union*; Phil Dahl-Bredine, *Instituto Paz en las Americas*; Kathy Engel, *Riptide Communications*; M. Patricia Fernández Kelly, *Johns Hopkins University*; Don Hancock, *Southwest Research and Information Center*; Carlos Heredia, *Equipo Pueblo*; Luis Hernández, *Coordinadora Nacional de Organizaciones Cafetaleras*; Patricia Hynds, *Latin America Database*; Claudia Isaac, *UNM Community and Regional Planning Program*; Antonio Lujan, *Diocese of Las Cruces*; Mary MacArthur, *The Diversity Project;* Jennifer Manríquez, *Albuquerque Technical-Vocational Institute*; Carmen Alicia Nebot, *United Church of Christ*; Debra Preusch, *Resource Center*; Margaret Randall, *Writer and Photographer*; Michael Ratner, *Center for Constitutional Rights*; Primitivo Rodríguez, *Universidad Nacional Autónoma de México*; Frank I. Sánchez, *New Mexico Community Foundation*; Moises Sandoval, *Journalist*; Beth Wood, *Community Activist*. (Organizations listed for identification purposes only.)

Become an RC member!

Yes! I want to support your efforts to make the U.S. a responsible member of the world community.

☐ **$25 Basic Membership:** You receive one year (four issues) of our quarterly *Resource Center Bulletin*.

☐ **$50 Amiga/Amigo Membership:** You receive subscriptions to the *Bulletin*, bimonthly *Democracy Backgrounder*, monthly *BorderLines*, and all our special reports.

☐ **$100 Compañera/Compañero Membership:** You receive all our periodicals, special reports, and a 33% discount on RC books.

☐ **$250 Comadre/Compadre Membership:** You receive all the benefits of a compañera membership as well as all new RC materials free.

☐ **$1,000 RC Sustainer:** You receive all new publications, and you may take your pick of existing materials from our catalog.

Charge my ☐ VISA ☐ MasterCard

Account # _____

Expiration date _____ Daytime Phone (___)_____

Name_____

Street Address_____

City_____ State_____ Zip_____

The Interhemispheric Resource Center is a 501(c)3 nonprofit organization. All donations are tax deductible to the extent allowable by law.

☐ Please do not trade my name with other organizations.

To receive our catalog, write us or give us a call:

Interhemispheric Resource Center
P.O. Box 4506
Albuquerque, NM 87196
phone: (505) 842-8288
fax: (505) 246-1601

Central America

GUATEMALA
1992   308 pp.
ISBN 0-911213-40-6
$11.95

BELIZE
1995   200 pp.
ISBN 0-911213-54-6
$11.95

HONDURAS
1994   200 pp.
ISBN 0-911213-49-X
$11.95

COSTA RICA
1995   200 pp.
ISBN 0-911213-51-1
$11.95

EL SALVADOR
1995   304 pp.
ISBN 0-911213-53-8
$11.95

PANAMA
1995   160 pp.
ISBN 0-911213-50-3
$11.95

NICARAGUA
1990   226 pp.
ISBN 0-911213-29-5
$9.95

Everything you need to know about each nation's economy, politics, environment, and society.

SPECIAL OFFER

Buy all 7 books
for
$64.75
That's a savings
of $22.90!
(INCLUDES POSTAGE
AND HANDLING)
PRICES SUBJECT TO CHANGE

PREPAYMENT IS REQUIRED. INCLUDE $3.00 FOR THE
FIRST ITEM YOU ORDER; ADD 50¢ FOR EACH ADDITIONAL.
SEND CHECK OR MONEY ORDER PAYABLE TO:
Resource Center
Box 4506
Albuquerque, NM 87196

VISA/MASTERCARD ORDERS ACCEPTED BY PHONE
(505) 842-8288

ZAPATA'S REVENGE

Free Trade and the Farm Crisis in Mexico

by Tom Barry

The past and future collide in this compelling account of the drama unfolding in the Mexican countryside. Visions of a modernized and industrialized nation competing in the global market clash with the sobering reality of a desperate peasantry and falling agricultural production. These crises in Chiapas are the same ones confronting most of Mexico and the third world.

Barry views the crisis that confronts Mexico as alarming evidence of the incapacity of today's neoliberal and free trade policies to foster broad economic development. He explains that such strategies have resulted in reduced food security, environmental destruction, increased rural-urban polarization, depopulation of peasant communities and social and political instability.

This book offers personal interviews, investigative research, and analysis that goes to the heart of the development challenge faced by Mexico and other Latin American nations.

South End Press, 1995
ISBN 089608-499-X

250 PAGES
$16.00 paper

$35.00 cloth